THE SOCIAL HISTORY OF EDUCATION

GENERAL EDITOR: VICTOR E. NEUBURG

Second Series — No. 5

LITERACY AND SOCIETY

THE SOCIAL HISTORY OF EDUCATION

General Editor: Victor E. Neuberg

Second Series

No. 1. Sir Thomas Bernard

Of the Education of the Poor (1809)

No. 2. Eighteenth Century Education: Selected Sources

Edited by Victor E. Neuburg
The five pamphlets included in this volume exemplify eighteenth century approaches to popular education. They include a facsimile of one of the more important reading primers used in charity schools, an early manual of their organization and a highly significant sermon preached by Joseph Butler, Bishop of Bristol. An Appendix contains some useful material on reading methods.

No. 3. G. Griffith

Going to Markets and Grammar Schools, 2 vols (1870)

No. 4. A. Hill (Editor)

Essays Upon Educational Subjects (1857)

No. 5. Literacy and Society

Comprising:
Introduction by Victor E. Neuburg

  (i) W. H. Reid: *The Rise and Dissolution of Infidel Societies in this Metropolis . . . etc. (1800)*

  (ii) W. J. Linton: *James Watson. A Memoir of the days of the fight for a free press, 2nd edition (1880)*
Appendix
Catalogue of James Watson's publications

No. 6. Nineteenth Century Education: Selected Sources

Edited by Victor E. Neuburg
The subjects included in this selection cover Penny Readings, Ragged Schools, the training of working women and working class recreations; as well as a contemporary biography of J. G. Brooks who undertook much voluntary educational work.

No. 7. J. A. St. John

The Education of the People (1858)

No. 8. J. C. Symons

School Economy (1852)

LITERACY AND SOCIETY
Edited with a new introduction by Victor E. Neuburg

THE

RISE AND DISSOLUTION

OF THE

INFIDEL SOCIETIES

IN THIS METROPOLIS

BY

WILLIAM HAMILTON REID

Together with

JAMES WATSON

A MEMOIR

OF THE DAYS OF THE FIGHT FOR A FREE PRESS
IN ENGLAND AND OF THE AGITATION FOR THE
PEOPLE'S CHARTER

BY

W. J. LINTON

WITH AN APPENDIX CONTAINING A CATALOGUE OF
JAMES WATSON'S PUBLICATIONS

THE WOBURN PRESS

1971

Published by

WOBURN BOOKS LIMITED

10 Woburn Walk, London WC1 0JL

The Rise and Dissolution of the Infidel Societies
in this Metropolis

First edition   1800
New impression   1971

James Watson—A Memoir

First edition   1800
New impression   1971

ISBN 0 7130 0014 7

Printed in Great Britain by Clarke, Doble & Brendon Ltd.
Plymouth and London

NEW INTRODUCTION

By the end of the eighteenth century the ability to read had become widespread amongst the English poor; and this achievement of at least some degree of literacy was to prove an important factor in the re-ordering of society which followed the Industrial Revolution.

Two very different kinds of enterprise which had gathered momentum throughout the century provided the means by which many of the poor had learned their letters. In the first place, elementary education became widely available in Charity Schools— and it could also, of course, be acquired in the humble establishments which were run by individuals who charged a small weekly sum for the very basic teaching which they offered. Such education usually provided extremely limited scope for exercising a skill in reading; but, by way of nourishment for this skill, there existed in chapbooks a genuinely popular literature, entirely secular in character, which increased in volume as the century progressed. These chapbooks, produced in London and the provinces by a large number of printers and publishers, and sold by pedlars who travelled, pack on back, the length and breadth of the country, were within reach of all by reason both of their wide distribution and of their very small cost.

From these small beginnings the effects upon the structure of society were to be far-reaching, and a clear pointer to this is the fact that by the turn of the century the artisan could be reading a cheap edition of Thomas Paine's *Rights of Man*, and subject to the influence which such a reformer was liable to have upon him. To what extent did this reflect the objectives of those who had been concerned with the underprivileged and their place in society?

Charity Schools were the outcome of a philanthropic spirit which characterised the activities of the Society for Promoting Christian Knowledge in the years which followed its foundation in 1699. The theory which underlay its endeavours was a relatively simple one: society was seen as a divinely ordered mechanism in which everyone knew his place; and the poor, despite the grinding poverty and long hours of toil which were usually their lot, were expected to remain hardworking, submissive and content in the station of life to which God had called them. In order to perpetuate such a social framework it was held by members of the Society, and other 'reformers' like Isaac Watts and Hannah More, that the poor should be taught to read so that the Bible and other suitable religious works would be available to them, and enable them to confirm for themselves the necessity of remaining pious, docile and grateful to their betters. In this way, it was felt, the existing social pattern would be maintained.

On the other hand, many voices were raised to advocate that the poor should be left in ignorance. "What ploughman who could read . . . would be content to whistle up one furrow and down another, from dawn in the morning, to the setting of the sun?", asked George Hadley in 1786—a question which really epitomised the views of all those who were resolutely opposed to modifying the ignorance of the labouring classes. How indeed could they remain content with their lot if they had access to books? What was to prevent them, once they could read, from turning not to the Bible and to other suitable religious works, but to chapbooks and to other infidel publications?

And history proved them right. Ironically, those whose work we can applaud in the foundation of Charity Schools and other agencies of elementary education for the underprivileged, in the belief that by so doing they were ensuring the continuance of the established order, found their motives confounded; for the philanthropic condescension of the privileged towards the less fortunate members of society became increasingly less relevant as the artisan found himself able to turn to the *Rights of Man*, and began to feel himself a member of the emergent working class. The mould had been shattered.

W. H. Reid, author of the first book reprinted here, attributed the spread of infidel ideas very largely to the incidence of reading, and the picture he draws, while it may be in some respects an exaggerated one, does indicate the deep concern which was felt in some quarters about the fact that so many of the poor were able to read. In 1803, some three years after the appearance of Reid's book, an eight-page pamphlet, issued without a publisher's name and entitled "Popular and Patriotic Tracts", listed upwards of seventy publications ranging in price from ½d. to 3d. each, with special prices for orders in bulk intended "for Distribution". The unknown author—presumably the publisher—said on the first page:

"The dissemination of these in the Metropolis, and its vicinity, has already produced the happiest effects . . ." The most important of these was described as "HARMONY among OURSELVES". These tracts, clearly intended as an antidote to the pernicious influences, radicalism and unbelief which many felt were reaching the poor through the medium of the printed word, serve to substantiate the views presented by Reid.

If W. H. Reid deplored the spread of literacy, James Watson, publisher of political and freethinking material some years later, did much to exploit it. He was, it is true, not the first to do so. Richard Carlile had already made a name for himself both as publisher and as editor of books, pamphlets and periodicals which brought him into conflict with the law. Watson, indeed, was connected with Carlile in 1822, and as a result can have had few illusions about the difficulties which faced a publisher or bookseller who propagated views that were unacceptable to the Government of the day. Despite such hazards, Watson made available as cheaply as possible a very wide range of heterodox publications*, and his shop in Paul's Alley was well known.

Reid's view represents perhaps the last word of the eighteenth century upon the problem of reading and the poor. It was too late when he was writing to put back the clock, and he could only lament the appearance of what he regarded as a subversive force in society. Watson, on the other hand, saw the ability to read as a means of propagating ideas. His achievement in this respect—essentially one which concerned the education of working men—has received very much less attention than the acrimonious struggle which was carried on by the Church of England and the Nonconformists over the control of these same working men's children and grandchildren.

1970   V.E.N.

* See Appendix for one of Watson's catalogues.

THE
RISE AND DISSOLUTION

OF THE

INFIDEL SOCIETIES

IN THIS METROPOLIS:

INCLUDING,

THE ORIGIN OF MODERN DEISM AND ATHEISM;
THE GENIUS AND CONDUCT OF THOSE
ASSOCIATIONS; THEIR LECTURE-
ROOMS, FIELD-MEETINGS,
AND DEPUTATIONS;

From the Publication of PAINE's AGE OF REASON till
the present Period.

Φάσκοντες εἶναι σοφοὶ, ἐμωράνθησαν.　　ST. PAUL.

WITH

General Considerations on the Influence of Infidelity upon
Society; answering the various Objections of Deists
and Atheists; and a Postscript upon the present
State of Democratical Politics; Remarks
upon Professor Robison's late
Work, &c. &c.

By WILLIAM HAMILTON REID.

LONDON:

PRINTED FOR J. HATCHARD, BOOKSELLER TO HER
MAJESTY, NO. 173, PICCADILLY.

1800.

INTRODUCTION

THE Reader is candidly informed, that the mention of *Infidel Societies*, by the Bishop of London, in his late excellent charge, was a forcible motive for digesting the narrative contained in this work. After the enumeration of its contents, in the title-page, it is scarcely necessary to insist upon this new and important æra, herein described: *new*, because it delineates the first period in which the doctrines of Infidelity have been extensively circulated among the lower orders; and *important*, because the trial they have had, as it will appear in the sequel, has decidedly pronounced upon their weakness, and absolute incapacity to ameliorate or improve the state and condition of mankind.

Professor Robison and the Abbé Barruel, it is acknowledged, have given an interesting account of similar societies in France and Germany,

many, previous to the late revolution; but if these are to be regarded as an illustration of the monition

" Nam tua res agitur paries cum proximus ardet,"

the firing of a neighbour's house shall be esteemed trivial indeed, in comparison with a mine that was ready to burst our under feet! With the existence of these English affiliations, it is probable, that, few of the higher orders were acquainted; but their extensive influence and energies, certainly communicate a degree of interest to the detail here given, as the first account of them.

The Author of this undertaking, having been involved in the dangerous delusion he now explodes, may reasonably be admitted a competent witness of the events which he relates; as may also the presumption, that he has demonstrated the impracticability of the Infidel scheme, not merely from speculation, to which former writers have been confined, but from facts deduced from real life and actual experience.

Like our predecessors, we are then no longer under the necessity of arguing without a living precedent; on the contrary, we have seen the
principles

principles of Infidelity transferred from *books* to *men*; from *dead* characters to *living* subjects; not among a few isolated or speculative individuals, but in numerous and compact bodies.

What was formerly a dispute, is thus brought upon a new ground; and from the heterogeneous composition of this upstart body, the question " Whether a Society of Atheists can " subsist ?" it is presumed, may now be decided in the negative.

Agreeable to this statement, Mr. Robert Hall, of Cambridge, in the preface to his Sermon intituled, *Modern Infidelity confidered, &c.* observes, that the cotroversy between Infidels and Christians *appears to have taken a new turn :* the influence of Infidelity upon society, he says is a point hitherto little confidered. The present exposure of these opinions, by one who has witnessed their most secret operations; and the most unqualified expression of the views of those who espoused them, may awaken the rancour of Infidel fanatics; but this he presumes, will be more than counter balanced by the approbation of the learned and soberminded of all Christian denominations. As for the probable defects of this work, in point of
ftyle,

ftyle, or in the art of compofition, my apology
to the learned is, that it was written upon the
fpur of the occafion, and *currente calamo.*

Perhaps the relative obfcurity of thefe affiliations may have been the reafon they were
not fooner noticed; as, in refpect to their lo-
cality in this metropolis, it muft be confeffed
they bear fome refemblance with the Parifian
Fauxbourgs of St. Antoine, &c.

After the faithful delineation of facts, in
this work, it is hoped, Infidels will no longer
claim the character of Philofophers! If Philofophy has any connection with the conduct of
the human mind, towards the *Chief-good*, it is
not the Infidel, but the rational Chriftian,
who has the beft right to that high diftinction;
for, " the man who happily unites Philofophy
with Religion, is the dupe, neither of fcepticifm, fuperftition, or fanaticifm."

Were I at liberty to mention *feveral eminent
literary characters*, who have honoured this
work with their attention, while in manu-
fcript, it might be conftrued into an attempt
to bias the public opinion; but, till that decifion is pronounced, the Author alone, is refponfible for the whole; I am therefore " ready

to

to prove any thing I have ftated, if called upon."

Quod fcripfi, fcripfi.

The importance of the fubject at large, might have been enhanced by fuperior abilities; but relative to its religious truths, I am not afraid of concluding with the exulting ftrains of the Roman Poet:

Jam exegi quod nec Jovis ira, nec ignes,
Nec potuit ferrum, nec edax abolere vetuftas.

THE

RISE AND DISSOLUTION, &c.

CHAP. I.

Upon some remote and the immediate Causes of the late Rise and Progress of Infidelity.—Patronage of the Age of Reason by the London Corresponding Society.—Mirabaud's System De la Nature.— Volney's Ruins of Empires.—Conversion of the Division-Rooms into the Mediums of Infidelity.

To suppose the late inclination to infidelity, to have been the result of cool inquiry, or rational conviction, would be a grofs libel upon the good fenfe of the country. On the contrary, the moft prominent reafon which can be given for this new propenfity is, that the public mind was taken by furprize, merely through the medium by which the evil complained of was obtruded by a certain fociety, affifted by the politics of the moment.

With thefe politics, it was fuppofed the new religion would blend and unite ; and to the mif-

applied

applied zeal of this fociety, and its partizans out of
doors, the fhort-lived increafe of thofe opinions
was owing.

Still there were other caufes which, though
feemingly remote, had an immediate effect upon
the minds of many who were waiting to avail
themfelves of any public event to promote a particular object. It being a general tradition among
Proteftants, that the feat of the Roman Catholic
religion was to be annihilated, it unfortunately
occurred, that, as the French were fuccefsful, after
the period of the revolution, in defpoiling that
church, notwithftanding their general efpoufal of
infidelity, their admirers ftill fuppofed them to be
the *inftruments* of fulfilling their favourite predic-
tion; and were fo much the eafier perfuaded to
adopt French principles in religion, while they
excufed the perpetrators of deeds, at which they
could not but fhudder, under the idea that the former were the felect *agents* of Providence; and thus,
from the dereliction of one religious denomination,
they were led, by an eafy gradation, to wifh for the
deftruction of all the reft.

From hence, under the idea of the inftrumenta-
lity of the French revolution, in the fulfilment of
prophecies, religion itfelf became acceffary to
deifm and atheifm! Prophecies, relative to the deftruction of almoft every kingdom and empire in
the world, teemed from the Britifh prefs, fome of
them in weekly numbers, till government, perfectly aware of the tendency of thefe inflammatory
means, prudently transferred the prince of prophets
to a mad-houfe.

It was natural for infidels, who had a revolution
in view, to connive at thofe enthufiafts who believed
in vulgar predictions relative to the deftruction of
Popery; it was natural alfo for the former to embrace
                                              fuch

fuch converts; but the attachment they obtained from thofe characters, who had the leaft remains of true religion, was of very fhort duration; as the general habit of ridiculing every thing before held facred, frequently created difguft, and occafioned a revolt from a party, who, notwithftanding all their profeffions about a *general* improvement of the morals of men, could not conceal the little value they fet upon *perfonal reformation!* juft as if the aggregate of fociety was not made up of individuals. In fact, to have hinted any thing relative to religious impreffions, though with all the modifications of a Socinian, would have ftigmatized its author as a mere ideot, or driveller, among thefe modern fages and pretended reformers. The Rev. Henry Kett, in his ftriking application of the Scriptures in his *Hiftory, the beft Interpreter of Prophecy,* feems to impute too little to the fecret and almoft imperceptible operations of Infidelity through the whole courfe of the laft century, efpecially in the interval between the publication of Bolingbroke's works, and the year 1776. This hiatus, not to keep my readers from the contemplation of more recent danger, I fhall endeavour to fupply in my poftfcript, only obferving at prefent, as the immediate caufe of the late rife and progrefs of infidelity, that an Englifhman in Paris, the head of a political party here, probably wifhing to revive his popularity in France, produced that laft effort of religious Quixotifm, the Age of Reafon. The early predilection of the London Correfponding Society for this performance, was the fole medium which, for the firft time, made infidelity as familiar as poffible with the lower orders. But the experiment thus tried, inftead of confolidating the wild theory of its authors, has only furnifhed their

Chriftian

Chriftian opponents with the ftrongeft grounds of objeftion.

It may now be faid, that the fplendid theories of Voltaire have been reduced to praftice ; the impaffioned eloquence of John James Rouffeau applied to the objefts defignated by its author ; and that the pertnefs and fcurrility of Thomas Paine have been added : but all thefe efforts have been, and will ftill be found illufory, as will farther appear from a faithful ftatement of recent events, and fuch reflettions as naturally refult therefrom.

If the fafts I am about to adduce were not well warranted, pofterity would not believe, that in confequence of the publication of a rhapfody againft the doftrines of Chriftianity, hazarded by a theoretical politician in 1794, and under favour of the French revolution, a very confiderable number of our countrymen adopted his notions ; and became equally as violent for the extermination of the Chriftian religion, as for the remedy of thofe *civil abufes*, for which alone their fociety was at firft eftablifhed !

Without experience of the faft, who would believe that while the infatuated difciples of the new philofophy were declaiming againft their clergy, for mingling politics with religion, they themfelves, employed miffionaries to add deifm to the democracy of their converts ! Or, who would credit that every religious obligation, in civilized fociety, was refifted as prieftcraft, by the fame perfons who were the loudeft in their demands, for what they chofe to difguife with the name of a reform !

Perhaps this mania, in its firft appearance, may be attributed to an implicit belief in moft of its advocates, that the new philofophy would·produce better effefts upon the manners of fociety, than

the

the religion of their forefathers had done. But how ftrongly the *practice* of the philofophers has belied the *theory*, will evidently appear in the impartial examination of their public conduct, which, as propagandifts, would have been much more alarming, had their fecret activity been appreciated fooner.

It is ftill fair to admit, that the adoption of Paine's Age of Reafon was not agreed, to in the London Correfponding Society, without confiderable oppofition, efpecially in the general committee; but as zeal fuperfeded judgment, in their difcuffions upon the fubject, the epithets of d-m--d fool, and d-m--d Chriftian, ultimately prevailed; and a bookfeller was foon perfuaded, by the heads of the party, to undertake a cheap edition of the Age of Reafon, for its more ready diffemination through the divifions, at that time rapidly increafing in number every week: but after Williams, the bookfeller juft alluded to, was imprifoned for this publication, his family received much lefs affiftance from the fociety, than from mere ftrangers.

In the hour of its admiration, this rhapfody was ridiculoufly termed the *New Holy Bible;* a circumftance which fully evinced the intentions of Mr. Paine's partizans: in fine, the attachment of the party was carried fo far, that the bare circumftance of having the Age of Reafon in a houfe, was deemed a collateral proof of the *civifm* of the poffeffor.

It may be urged, that this conduct of the fociety was never juftified by any act of the body at large: this is granted; but when it is confidered, that their inclination for deifm was fufficiently powerful to occafion a fchifm, which produced a *new fociety,*

under

under the denomination of the *Civil* and *Religious;* it follows, that the preponderance of a party, in the original body, was equal to a decision of the whole, and fixes the charge of a partiality to infidelity, beyond the possibility of a doubt.

If farther proofs were wanting, I might urge the circumstance of the establishment of a test, by the newly formed body, in which, each member acknowledged the *belief of the Holy Scriptures, and that Christ is the Son of God;* and this as a necessary qualification for their admission. This fact alone, I presume, would be sufficient for my purpose; to which may be added, that Bone and Lee, two seceding members, and booksellers by profession, were *proscribed* for refusing to sell Volney's Ruins, and Paine's Age of Reason; and that refusal construed into a censure upon the weakness of their intellects. Still, nothing like a miraculous conversion of the London Corresponding Society is to be imputed to Mr. Paine's Anti-theological Work. On the contrary, their minds were prepared for this more popular performance, by the more learned and elaborate productions of Mirabaud's System of Nature, and Volney's Ruins of Empires: the latter, in point of style, is looked upon as the Hervey of the Deists; the former, as the Newton of the Atheists: and, as the System of Nature was translated by a person confined in Newgate as a patriot, and published in weekly numbers, its sale was pushed, from the joint motive of serving the Author, and the cause in which the London Corresponding Society were engaged.

Northcote's Life of David was also reprinted in a very small edition; and if this vehicle for degrading the Bible had been better received, it was in agitation to biographize all the leading characters

ters in the Old and New Teftaments, as the moft
certain means of bringing the Chriftian religion
into contempt.

Propofals were circulated for reprinting the
whole works of Peter Annet ; much being expected from the plainnefs of his ftyle, and his mode of
reafoning againft revelation by fcriptural quota-
tions ; but, owing to the dread of a profecution,
not more than three weekly numbers, at three-
halfpence each, made their appearance. The
Rights and Duties of Citizenfhip, moft remarkable
for copying the blunders of Voltaire, was one of
the laft things, of this kind, ufhered into public
view ; but being profecuted, and the publifhers
fentenced to two years folitary imprifonment, a
final ftop was put to this mode of promoting fcepticifm and infidelity.

The Beauties of Deifm ; A Moral Dictionary ;
Julian againft Chriftianity ; and, laftly, that para-
gon of French Atheifm, LE BON SENS, *Ou Idées
Naturelles oppofes aux Idées Surnaturelles*, were in
agitation to have followed. The latter, for its audacity and virulence, has poffibly never been furpaffed, and its laft fection is probably no bad fum-
mary of the whole.

" La religion, n'a fait en tout tems que rem-
" plir l'efprit de l'homme de tenebres et le retenir
" dans l'ignorance de fes vrais rapports, de fes
" vrais devoirs, de fes interêts véritables. Ce n'eft
" qu'en ecartant fes nuages et fes phantômes que
" nous decouvrirons les fources du vrai, de la
" raifon, de la morale, & les motifs reels qui doi-
" vent nous porter à la vertu. Cette religion nous
" donne le change, & fur les caufes de nos maux
" & fur les remedes naturels que nous pourrions
" y appliquer : loin de les guerir, elle ne peut
" que les aggraver, les multiplier, & les rendre
                                                " plus

" plus durables. Difons donc avec un celebre
" moderne, *la Theologie eft la boite de Pandore;*
" *& s'il eft impoffible de la refermer, il eft au-*
" *moins utile d'avertir que cette boete fi fatale eft*
" *ouverte.*"

Impregnated with the principal objections of all
the infidel writers, and big with the fancied importance of being inftrumental in a general reform,
almoft every divifion-room could now boaft its advocate for the new philofophy. In fact, fuch a
torrent of abufe and declamation appeared to burft
from all quarters at once, that as the idea of a
Deift and a good *Democrat* feemed to have been
univerfally compounded, very few had the courage
to oppofe the general current. On the other hand,
feveral perfons really facrificed their private fentiments to the public opinion, merely to avoid the
contempt every where beftowed upon thofe who
dared to open their mouths in defence of principles
and opinions, till then held facred.

Next to fongs, in which the clergy were a ftanding fubject of abufe ; in conjunction with pipes
and tobacco, the tables of the club-rooms were
frequently ftrewed with penny, two-penny, and
three-penny publications, as it were fo many fwi-
vels againft eftablifhed opinions ; while, to enable
the members to furnifh themfelves with the heavy
artillery of Voltaire, Godwin, &c. reading-clubs
were formed. But ftill, fo it happened, that thofe
who defpifed the labour of reading, took their
creeds implicitly, from the extemporaneous effufions of others, whofe talents were comparatively
above their own. And yet thefe people were invariably in the habit of ridiculing Chriftians, in
concert with the orators, for being blindly led by
priefts.

After

After thefe notions of infidelity were in a manner eftablifhed in the divifions, it is natural to fuppofe, that in choofing their delegates, thofe pérfons were preferred who were doubly recommended by *their religion*, and their politics; in faƈt, this was fo prevalent, that in the recommendation of any perfon to an office among them, it was common to diftinguifh him as " *A good Democrat* " *and a Deift.*" Or, to fix the charaƈter more ftrongly, to add, " *That he is no Chriftiun.*"

However, from this period, when the leaders began to force their anti-religious opinions upon their co-affociates, it is undeniable that their inteftine divifions haftened their diffolution more than any external obftacles.

I fhall now proceed to a detail of the recent places of rendezvous, as they were held by thefe perturbed fpirits, which, I hope, will not be deemed trivial. The once famed Robin Hood Society had feveral hiftorians in profe and verfe; and yet, unlike its fucceffors, it combined no *political* with its fo-called *religious* views. In its decline alone it bore the moft refemblance to the modern clubs, in the defeƈtion of many of its beft members, when the confequences of their difcuffions, aƈting upon the public morals, appeared to them in a different light from what they feemed at firft.

CHAP.

CHAP. II.

Of various new Societies, Field-Meetings, and Deputations.—Their Conduct and Progress.— Violence of the Clubbists against the Clergy.— Effects of their Enthusiasm upon their Auditors. —Propagandists in the Benefit and Convivial Societies.

ONE of the first of these associations was fixed in the club-room of the Green Dragon, in Fore-street, near Cripplegate, in the spring of 1795. That apartment was then occupied by a Reading Society, which was soon swallowed up in the vortex of the ensuing debate, and was so much crowded, in a very short time, as to render an entrance, as well as respiration, extremely difficult.

That no opportunity might be lost, a question, subversive of the Christian religion, was also agitated, in the same room, on a Wednesday evening; but being very thinly attended, it was found necessary to pay both the speakers and president, out of the money collected from the audience.

On the other hand, the debate on a Sunday evening always drew a crowded audience, during a twelvemonth, in which it was continued at that house; when, upon the complaint of some of the neighbours, that the landlord kept bad hours, (as the disputes above and below stairs seldom terminated before one in the morning) they were compelled to leave the premises, to prevent worse consequences to the keeper of the house.

Their

Their fittings were afterwards alternately held at a houfe in Windmill-ftreet, Finfbury-fquare; and at the George, in Eaft Harding-ftreet, Fetter-lane, which, being a very commodious room, the noife made by the clapping of the fpeakers, and the late hours kept by the company, occafioned a complaint, that, being immediately attended to, by a worthy officer of the ward, not far from the fpot, the club was removed to the Fountain, in Fetter-lane, and again hunted from its new retreat, till they ultimately fettled at the Scots Arms, in Little Britain, and were as numeroufly attended as at any former period: here they continued the greateft part of the winter of 1797, but being compelled to leave it, through the magiftrate's interference, the landlord was afterwards deprived of his licence for entertaining them. Its next ftage of exiftence was at the Golden Key, near Moor-lane, Moor-fields; but here it attracted fo great a concourfe of attendants, that the landlord, dreading the confequences, warned them away: this was alfo the cafe at another houfe, near Union-ftreet, Moorfields; till, adjoining to the Britifh Wine-houfe, near Hoxton, beyond the limits of the city-officers, they carried on their difquifitions, near two months, without meeting with any new embarrafment.

In the interval, between the fpring of 1795 and the period laft fpoken of, feveral other fo-cieties, upon a fmaller fcale, had been fet on foot: one of thefe, the next, in point of promife, to that of the Green Dragon, was intitled, " The Moral and Political Society," who, like the former, converted their place of meeting, near Bunhill-row, into a Debating-room. A few revolutionary pamphlets, written and printed at the fociety's expence,

expence, were publiſhed, during the interval to which I have alluded.

Similar meetings were alſo held at a public houſe, near Grub-ſtreet; and another, near the quarters of Moorfields.

Another, and one of the laſt places of any note for the exhibition of infidelity, in the eaſtern diſtrict, was at a Hair-dreſſer's in the High-ſtreet, Shoreditch, where a theological queſtion was debated, on a Sunday evening; but, as no money was taken at the door, the law, then in force, was evaded

Several other ſmall branches ſpread themſelves in the neighbourhood of Whitechapel, Spital-fields, and Hoxton; but were not of ſufficient notoriety, or duration, to merit much attention.

The Weſt end of the metropolis, having in the mean while attained to a degree of rivalſhip, in conſequence of an aſſociation, in Wells-ſtreet, Oxford-road, where the members were permitted to recite their own productions; and another, on a Sunday evening, much more numerouſly attended, viz. the Angel, in Cecil-court, St. Martin's Lane. Thoſe neareſt the city were, in ſome meaſure, deſerted; but, as they cloſed their debates ſooner than thoſe at the weſt end of the town, ſome of the ſpeakers contrived to exhibit at two places on the ſame night: even the weather preſented but few obſtacles. The viſionary expectation of a new order of things, it is preſumed, often vibrated from the imaginations of the leading members to their fingers ends, and rendered them leſs ſenſible of the operations of the elements than the vulgar herd.

The Wells-ſtreet Society being diſſolved, in conſequence of ſome diſagreement among the members, the whole focus of Deiſm and Atheiſm
was

was concentrated at the Angel, in Cecil-court,
St. Martin's Lane, where a mingled difplay of
real talent and miferable imitation was continued,
on the Sunday and Wednefday evenings, till Februry, 1798; when, without any previous notice
from the Weftminfter-magiftrates, as had been
cuftomary in the city, a period was put to this
promifing fchool; the whole of the members, *and
others* prefent, being apprehended, and, the next
day, obliged to find fureties for their appearance,
to anfwer any complaint, at the next Quarter-
Seffion, at Guildhall, Weftminfter; but no bill
being found, the bufinefs ended with the withdrawing of the recognizances of the parties, 57
in number; which would certainly have been
doubled, if the police-officers, fent to apprehend
the club, had ftayed till the bufinefs of the evening
had commenced.

This meeting was then deemed wholly political!
an idea which could have no other foundation
than the filly appellation of *citizen*, made ufe of
by the members; or the circumftance of its being
attended by John Binns, who was apprehended
about the fame period this fociety was difturbed,
in company with Arthur O'Connor, in Kent. This
unexpected ftroke of juftice, however, put the laft
hand to the Sunday-night meetings; at the weft
end of the town; the affociators in that quarter,
after holding a few thin fittings, at a houfe near
Compton-ftreet, Soho, being completely difperfed.
Previous to the eftablifhment of the club at this
place, another had been continued a confiderable
time, on a Wednefday evening, at a public houfe,
the corner of Long-Acre, oppofite Newport-Mar-
ket. Here, as well as at the other places, the
queftions agitated were partly religious, and partly
political.

In

In all thefe places, where anti-religious opinions were ftated, it was furprifing to obférve how ftrongly their novelty attracted the public mind. The perfection to which the orators had attained, by a long practice, was fuch, that had commodious apartments been opened in any of the neighbourhoods, occupied by working people, their can be no doubt of their commanding large auditories. The zeal and energy of the fpeakers, as there were few, very few, whofe judgement was matured by time, had alfo great weight in making converts; for, among the lower orders of people, an extemporaneous harangue, againft the minifters of religion, had an effect not eafily imagined. This was particularly noticeable about Spitalfields, when, as the French fyftem of politics infenfibly attached itfelf to the auxiliary ideas of prophefies, fulfilling on the Continent, it would be difficult to fay, where the effects would ·have ceafed, had time been given to obtain that confiftence wifhed for by the vifionary movers of thofe irritable bodies.

It may be objected, that thefe clubs were only frequented by low and obfcure characters; but fuch, it may be remembered, were Maffinello, the Fifherman of Naples, the Cobler of Meffina, and many others: though the objection does not altogether lie againft the focieties in queftion. They were, for a time, fanctioned by fome perfons above the common rank, by their fortunes and profeffions in life. Among thefe, a fingular character ufed to be remarked, ·being in the habit of attending in a large round hat, nearly the fize of an umbrella, bordered with gold-lace; and he had other eccentricities, which he ufed to vary according to caprice. And to fortune and talents, might be added, an enthufiafm capable of roufing
the

the moſt infenſate to act againſt what was
deemed a *ſpiritual tyranny,* in the compulſory
payment of church-rates, to the amount of a few
pence per week! A favourite theme with ſome of
the club-orators; with one of whom, it uſed to
be a common-place obſervation, that, " *There*
" *could not be a more awfuller ſight in the world,*
" *than to ſee a Biſhop rolling about in his cha-*
" *riot.*" Of another of theſe enthuſiaſts it was
mentioned, " That it was with difficulty he could
" reſtrain the moſt violent feelings, whenever the
" preſent Archbiſhop of Canterbury paſſed under
" his window." After theſe traits of club-cha-
racters, and among men with whom *private aſſaſ-
ſination* was looked upon as no crime, one might
think, that even what has been contemptuouſly
called the *pop-gun* plot did not deſerve that air
of incredibility and myſtery thrown upon it by
ſome writers.

Still as the reins were then held by government, very little was to be feared from any overt-
acts among theſe deſcriptions; though, if their
temporary ebullitions of zeal could be deemed a
fair criterion, this negative obedience might be
imputed more to a want of power than of will.
Vain glory, and a blind reſentment, as ſilly as
it is ſavage, often hurry men into the wildeſt extremes.—I am an Atheiſt! exclaimed one of thoſe
perſons, and, jumping upon a club-room table;
here, ſaid he, holding up an infant, here is a young
Atheiſt! Another, to ſhew how little he regarded
the Bible, obſerved, at another meeting, " That
" juſt before he came from home, he kicked ſome-
" thing before him, and, picking it up, what
" ſhould it be but an old Bible; that, till then,
" he did not know he had any ſuch thing in his
" houſe!" A third philoſopher, cenſuring the
preſent

prefent mode of education, obferved, " There " would never be any good done, till towns and " cities were built without a fingle church, cha- " pel, or any place of worfhip, in them!" Another member, being weary of the deliberations at which he was prefent, exclaimed, " *What fignifies our* " *fitting here? let us go and kill all the bl—dy* " *priefts!*"

I mention thefe inftances, only as the effects of a party fpirit, breathing fentiments by no means natural, but merely forced from the hot-beds of the clubs.

It fhould be obferved, that as apprentices were admitted into thefe affemblies; and, ac- cording to the modern notions of equality, eligi- ble to the chair; fo fudden a tranfition, from do- meftic inferiority to profeffional importance, often turned a weak head: and, if the fame extremities had been proceeded to as the religious fanatics of the laft age were engaged in, the London appren- tices might again have diftinguifhed themfelves, and the cry of *no king* followed that of *no bifhop,* as a natural confequence.

But in hinting at a parallel between modern democratic zeal and the fanaticifm of the fixteenth century; of the latter I ought to beg pardon.— A degree of monftrofity, fufficient to make any humanized being fhudder, feems to have been referved for the Englifh Clubbifts and *Anti-Reli- gionifts* of later times. — I allude to a common toaft, which ufed to be received among them with acclamation, *viz.*

" *May the laft King be ftrangled in the bowels of the* " *laft Prieft!!!*"

In afcribing fo much of this intemperate zeal to party-fpirit, youth, and inexperience, every candid

candid mind will acquit me of any charge of partiality or mifreprefentation. An obfervation of Mr. Neckar's may probably confirm the propriety of the prefent application, by exhibiting a ftriking fimilarity between the modern Freethinkers in France and thofe in England: " We " now reckon, fays he, among thofe who oppofe " a contemptuous fmile to religious opinions, a " multitude of young people, often incapable of " fupporting the moft trivial arguments; and who, " perhaps, could not connect two or three abftract " propofitions: thefe pretended philofophers art- " fully, and almoft perfidioufly, take advantage " of the firft flight of felf-love, to perfuade be- " ginners, that they are able to judge, at a glance, " of the ferious queftions which have eluded the " penetration of the moft exercifed thinkers."

Inftead then of reckoning, as many perfons have done, upon the total abolition of Chriftianity, and fondly anticipating the *acquirements* of the next generation, as wholly Infidel, it fhould have been made a queftion, Whether the prefent generation of the French will retain its Infidel principles after its judgment is matured, and the hey-day of revolutions has fubfided?

But, to return: at the fame time that all thefe energies were called forth in the clubs, it became another branch of the duty of the members, and their partizans, to attend, perplex, and harrafs, by all poffible means, the itinerant preachers, in the vicinity of town. For inftance, during the fummer, of 1797, a very formidable party were organized, and affembled, every Sunday morning, at feven o'clock, near the City-road: here, in confequence of the debates, forced upon the preachers or the hearers, feveral groupes of people would remain upon the ground till noon, giving an opportunity

portunity to the unwary paſſengers to become acquainted with the dogmas of Voltaire, Paine, and other writers, of whom they might have remained in ignorance; in faɛt, the fields were reſorted to, by the new reformers, upon the ſame principle as a ſportſman goes in queſt of game :—" We ſhall be ſure to find ſome Chriſtians in " the fields" was the ſtanding reaſon for theſe excurſions.

So indefatigable were theſe propagandiſts in their labours, that, beſides their attendance on the Sunday morning, in conſequence of which the groupes would remain till noon, they were again aſſembled from three or four in the afternoon; and, if the weather permitted, retained till eleven at night; and this not in one but various parts of the environs of this metropolis. The cavilling parties, engaged in this buſineſs, demurred at no diſtance of place; being as ready to attend at Hoxton, Hackney, or Hornſey, as at their own doors. One of theſe bodies, I was afterwards informed, uſed to meet, every Sunday morning, in a garden near Bethnal-green, and, after ſpending ſome time in reading and commenting upon Paine's Age of Reaſon, diſtributed themſelves for the purpoſes above-mentioned.

In fine, this oppoſition from Deiſts and Atheiſts was carried to ſuch extremes, that, in 1798, the magiſtrates were compelled to put a partial ſtop to field-preaching; till that period, as common and habitual in the eaſtern ſuburbs, as it had been in Moorfields, previous to the ereɛtion of Finſbury-ſquare. A meaſure prompted intirely, by the advantages taken by the Infidel party, to propagate their abſurd opinions with more effeɛt.

In addition to the redoubtable army beforementioned, marſhalled for every kind of attack, both

both within and beyond the fphere of the clubs, a number of ftraggling auxiliaries might be reckoned upon, who were drawn together by the noife and alarm of the Field-Difputants. Thefe confifted of Myftics, Muggletonians, Millennaries, and a variety of eccentric characters of different denominations: I call them auxiliaries, becaufe, their ridiculous mode of defending, or enforcing; their different tenets only increafed the objections to the Chriftian Belief, in the minds of thofe perfons before unhinged by the fubtleties of Infidels; and thus, unintentionally, an additional weight was thrown into the fcale of the common enemy, by thofe who had a zeal, but not according to knowledge. Among the latter, were two preachers, called *Jew-Quakers*, from the circumftance of their having but one beard between them; one fhaving the *upper*, the other the *under*, lip only: to thefe may be added, a Bird-catcher, and a Bafket-maker, both well known as Holders-forth, and, of courfe, having their admirers.

All thefe grotefque characters, the Deifts and Atheifts, juftly confidered as fo many Punchinellos, whom thofe who held the wires behind the fcenes might play off, as beft fuited their purpofe; a pofition which a fuperficial obferver might not immediately perceive: but I recollect an inftance, in the fummer of 1798, at the conclufion of a Field-fermon, when it was remarked, that, the Deifts did not oppofe the Arian preachers with the fame virulence as the Trinitarians. The full force of the obfervation was admitted, while it was urged, as a reafon for this forbearance, that, the Infidels confidered the Arians as doing a part of their bufinefs for them.

But befides the fields, and the divifion-rooms, the Infidel-propagandifts made ufe of another medium

dium for fpreading their principles, in which they were but too fuccefsful: this was in the various Benefit-Societies, within the circle of the metropolis. Here, after the bufinefs of the evening was over, the difciple of Paine was fure to introduce the fubject of religion; and, by thefe means, feveral copies of the Age of Reafon were circulated, from the reading of which many of its victims dated their *converfion.*

But this infiduous mode of introducing the Age of Reafon having been fuccefsfully refifted by fome of the Benefit-Societies, who have complained to the magiftrates of fuch diforderly members; the latter, finding their temporal interefts at ftake, and not being inclined, by the new philofophy, to facrifice *principle* for *intereft*, it is fuppofed, will act with more cunning in future; it being through diffimulation alone, and that kind of it, which a Chriftian would difdain, by which thefe obnoxious members have efcaped the erafement of their names from the books of the Society, and, perhaps, in more than one inftance, engaged the magiftrates to prevent their exclufion.

The introduction of democratic fongs was another part of the duty of thefe political miffionaries; but their talents were not confined to Benefit-Clubs, their bufinefs was to worm themfelves into convivial focieties of every kind; where, though fcufftles have frequently enfued, thefe delegates have often fucceeded in erecting a party, or an intereft, which, otherwife, would not have had an exiftence.

Upon the whole, the difgufting licentioufnefs, coarfenefs, and brutal indelicacy, too frequently apparent in thofe field-difputations, more than counteracted every degree of utility attending them. It has

has feveral times occurred, that, when two perfons, rather ferioufly inclined, have been difcuffing the attributes of the Deity, a third has abruptly interfered, with what he has fuppofed to have been a fhrewd queftion, *viz.* " How do you know there is any God at all ? "

Having now done with the delineation of thefe diftortured features of humanity, I fhall now proceed to give an account of the eftablifhment of a place of public inftruction ; always an important object with the Infidel Illuminati. The next chapter will therefore fhew how far that eftablifhment was founded upon a judicious or a fanatical eftimate.

CHAP.

CHAP. III.

Upon the opening of a Temple of Reafon in the Spring of 1796.

IT had long been a favourite idea of the Club-Orators, and Field-Miffionary Difputants, that exhibited upon a proper ftage of action, their eloquence would be irrefiftible. Favoured by the French Revolution, they fondly imagined the time, for the explo* of the whole fabric of Chriftianity, had at length arrived; and that, to convert all fects from the abfurdity of Chriftian notions, nothing was wanting but the opportunity which then prefented itfelf, for proclaiming the *beauties of nature,* and *unaffifted reafon* to the world at large. Flufhed with thefe expectations, a committee was felected to meet at a public houfe, in Jewin-ftreet; when, after a few adjourned fittings, being affifted by two gentlemen of the law, fomething like a fociety was organized; a fund adequate to the undertaking was depofited, and the name of the affociation agreed upon, to be that of the *Friends of Morality.* To keep up the fpirit of this inftitution, it was ordered, that no perfon fhould be admitted, unlefs known fome months, by more than one of the members, and that exclufion fhould follow any act of immorality; but in confequence of the trouble that feemed likely to enfue upon the adoption of this regulation, thefe modern Cato's were foon compelled

pelled to give up a meafure, at firft conceived to be indifpenfibly neceffary to fupport the character of this new eftablifhment.

It being juftly conceived that every member was not qualified to deliver lectures in public, it foon became an object of high debate, in the committee, whether the lecturers fhould or fhould not be paid for their labours. And as any refemblance to the allowance of a ftipend to a real or nominal fuperior was looked upon as rank fuperftition, or of arifto-cratic tendency, it required all the influence of the two lawyers, to induce the majority of the members to agree to a claufe in their articles, to allow half a guinea to each lecturer, by way of compen-fation for his trouble.

A committee of managers was alfo appointed; but a card and fome emblematic divice being found a neceffary appendage, an engraver belonging to the body was employed, who produced a plate, exhibiting Truth with a fpeculum in her hand, con-centrating her rays upon the figure of Error, recum-bent upon the ground. Some of the committee, whofe tafte was not congenial to the fine arts, thought the charge of half-a-guinea moft exorbitant, while others fuppofed that the artift, being a mem-ber, fhould have contributed the affiftance of his talents without fee or reward.

After feveral fruitlefs attempts to procure a com-modious place of meeting, owing to a variety of objections from the perfons applied to, Nichols's fale-room, in Whitecrofs-ftreet, being taken at a rent of twenty pounds per annum : by the contri-butions and labour of fome of the members, it was foon furnifhed with feats, a tribune, &c. Books being the next object ; to accommodate fuch per-fons as chofe to read before the Sunday lectures commenced, the members were called upon to
contribute

contribute their ſtock for the public good, particularly ſuch works as militated moſt ſtrongly againſt
Chriſtianity; but it ſo happened, for want of better
knowledge, that ſome of the books ſent into the
depoſitory, were written in its behalf! A circum-
ſtance ſomething like the conduct of ſome of the
rioters in 1780, who being called upon to go to
ſuch a houſe, as they were *Catholics* there, replied,
" What are Catholics to us? We are only againſt
" *Popery* !"

After this room was opened, and looked
upon, *bona fide*, as a Temple of Reaſon, the
opening being announced by the poſting of bills,
it was imagined that the ſuperiority of Infidelity
would inevitably appear. The hopes of the
leaders were equal to any thing, and ſome of them,
almoſt perſuaded themſelves, they were the very
perſons deſignated by Dr. Prieſtley, but a few
years before, for the important and momentous
purpoſe of ſetting fire to the train ſo long accumulating under the Eſtabliſhed Church, from the ſuc-
ceſſive contributions of inflammable matter, by
Arians, Socinians, and other Schiſmatics. From
this opinion, and the promiſing æra of preaching
the doctrines of Deiſm, &c. in the fields, which
was partly contemporary; an æra, which appeared
to have been reſerved for the year 1796, portentous
of the Millennium of Infidelity, and of which, the
newly-opened Temple of Reaſon was viewed as the
immediate forerunner. It was therefore not ſtrange
that the moſt active members ſhould expect to have
their names handed down to poſterity, as the re-
ſtorers of religious liberty, which was firſt to eradi-
cate ſuperſtition and ſlavery from this iſland, and
afterwards, ſupported by the French Revolution,
make the tour of Chriſtendom.

Reſpecting

Respecting the external economy of this new Temple, as the acts of prayer and praise were expreſſly excluded, the defects of ſolemnity or impreſſion upon the attendants may eaſily be conjectured. Simple as the worſhip of the Quakers, without their gravity, ſingularity in dreſs, &c. each perſon that mounted the roſtrum ſeemed rather to be trying his talents than employed in any ſerious undertaking; and, while the doctrines of the new philoſophy, as far as they related to morality, were much too general to ſuit any particular purpoſe, the feelings of the impartial hearer, who juſtly expected the *new* religion would ſuperſede the *old*, were invariably thoſe of ſurprize and diſappointment.

It was the endeavour of the moſt rational members, to confine the lecturers to the delivery of their ſentiments upon morality, abſtractedly, without reference to Chriſtianity, or any other ſyſtem: but this the majority of the members oppoſed, well perſuaded, that, deprived of the moſt copious themes of argument, or rather declamation, they would entirely loſe the command over the paſſions of their auditors, and, of courſe, become more inſipid and uninteresting than any of the profeſſions they were determined to condemn.

This being the temper of the chiefs of this new Temple of Reaſon, the lectures there delivered were generally compiled from the writings of Voltaire, David Williams, and other authors, diſtinguiſhed for their rancour or prejudices againſt Chriſtianity. As for the decorum, indiſpenſably neceſſary in every kind of worſhip, or public inſtruction, the ſtrangers that attended this inſtitution could not be leſs influenced by it, than the members themſelves; as, from the opening of the place, from ten in the morning till one, and

on

on the Sunday afternoon, till the moment of the commencement of the lectures, the time was invariably fpent in farcaftic or facetious converfation, acrofs the tables, between the members; and, from the noify approbation this entertainment occafionally produced, it was difficult to determine, whether amufement or aftonifhment preponderated in the minds of the audience at large.

As thefe boafted philofophers were ignorant of the force of motives, and of fuch doctrines as influence the minds of individuals, it was not unaccountable, that a laxity of attendance among the members foon produced a fimilar difpofition in ftrangers; fo that, notwithftanding the additional notice which the place attracted, in confequence of a difturbance by fome intruders, and the ftatement of their examination at one of the police offices, in fome of the daily papers, the fociety, finding all their declamations " wafted upon the defert air," at length agreed to fhut up the Temple till a more convenient feafon; for, at that period, it was not thought impoffible but that, in a few months, the preffure of external circumftances, and the co-operation of the New Apoftlefhip, might occafion the converfion of St. Paul's Cathedral into a Temple of Reafon! No one forefeeing, that, in the fummer of 1799, the Theophilanthropic Temple, at Paris, would fhare the fate of its humble imitator at Nichols's fale-room in Whitecrofs-Street, notwithftanding the fupport of Thomas Paine and other eminent characters.

Thefe uncontroled experiments upon the lower orders of fociety in this country, among whom credulity is ever the ftrongeft, muft completely invalidate the plea of Infidels againft the reftraint of the civil law, and the old pretence, that Chrifti-

anity

anity is obliged to the fecular arm for its fupport.

It may be afked, what power reftricted the Theophilanthropifts in the performance of their worfhip at Paris? The government was not only in
their favour, but the public mind had been training
for years for the reception of their notions, from
the writings of the whole tribe of French Atheifts,
in which, as Mr. Courtenay obferves, a conftella-
tion of genius feemed united. Thefe Atheiftical
tenets, he juftly remarked, were diffufed in every
fpecies of writing, and the dulcet poifon was
greedily imbibed in every part of Europe. The
moft poignant ridicule, the fineft fallies of wit, and
the moft brilliant traits of imagination, threw a
falfe luftre over this deceptious fyftem ; the pernicious dogmas of their fchool captivated the attention, and were conveyed to the heart in the en-
chanting page of a novel, amidft the feigned ad-
ventures and paffionate endearments of lovers.
But the luminous fcrutinizing genius of Montef-
quiou, the fplendid levity of Voltaire, the impaffioned and fafcinating eloquence of Roufleau, the
precifion and depth of D'Alembert, the bold and
acute inveftigations of Boulanger, the daring para-
doxical fpirit of Helvetius, the majeftic fublimity
of Buffon, the profound aftronomic refearches of
Baille, the captivating elegance of Marmontel,
and the impreffive condenfed thoughts of Diderot,
have not, as the gentleman concludes, "*unfettled the
confecrated opinions of ages*, nor fhaken the venerable gothic ftructure from its *very foundation*."
For, on the contrary, this many-twinkling meteor
of Infidelity, after blazing its hour, has paled before the milder radiance and commanding luftre of
the gofpel luminary, the doctrines of which, are
not extraneous, but congenial to human nature.

The

The new philofophy, it is granted, may adorn the head, but thefe ennoble the heart. This wifdom may be allowed to bear the impreffion of human reafon, but it will never pafs current with weak and wounded humanity! It is formidable in books, but contemptible in life: in argument ftrong; in practice weak: a coin which may be kept for fhew, but not for ufe : it is a counterfeit, and its detection, by the ftandard of experience, now enables us to fay, with a confidence approaching to mathematical demonftration, and oracular authenticity :

" Thou art weighed in the balance, and found wanting."

Yes, ye Atheifts, it is true that our minds were confined in a narrow region, while our imaginations were delighted with the fmiling heavens above, and the rich diverfity beneath. But what have we obtained of *you* in exchange ? To the fruitful, though bounded view of hill and dale, has fucceeded the immeafurable defert ! Amazement was our firft fenfation at the magnitude of the profpect ; but now our eyes are appalled, and our hearts ficken at the famenefs of the fcene. Here the heavens above are as brafs, and the earth as iron beneath our feet. Our ears are torn by the fcreaming of the bittern, or alarmed by the howling of the beafts of prey. *The voice of the turtle is not heard in this land, and the time for finging birds never comes.*

But again, to advert to the hiftory of this grand failure of Infidelity ; that the fatal experiment was not tried upon a much larger fcale, is not to be imputed to the want of will in the perfons engaged, but to the falutary prevention which originated in another quarter: for no fooner was the opening of the place laft defcribed known in the
country,

country, than a notice was given in that affembly, " That if any perfon, qualified as a teacher, could " make it convenient to leave town, a Society, at " one of the Weftern ports, could infure him from " 150*l.* to 200*l.* per annum." Nor is it ftraining any probability to fuppofe, that every affembly of this nature would eventually have formed itfelf into a political body, the confequences muft then have been obvious.

The projeƈt for diftributing the miffionaries of Deifm and Democracy about the country, it feems, had certainly been aƈted upon, to a certain degree, anterior to the period I have juft alluded to, when, as the Bifhop of London obferves in one of his Lordfhip's charges to his clergy, *that, to his know-ledge, the Age of Reafon had been circulated among the miners in Cornwall.* A degree of mifchievous induftry, unknown to the original propagandifts of the continent, whofe impious labours, as far as I have heard, terminated upon the *furface* of the *earth!* But of the former it may be faid,

" That when on earth they could no farther go,
" They fpread the mifchief in the realms below!"

CHAP. IV.

Upon the common Prejudices in Favour of Debating Clubs; and the immediate Influence of the late Affociations, upon the Families and Connections of their Members.

PERHAPS the long practice of agitating civil and religious fubjects, in various focieties, has lent too much ftrength to the hitherto prevailing opinion, that fuch verbal difcuffions did certainly tend to the eftablifhment of truth, and the detection of error. But fpeaking from long experience, at leaft, ever fince Infidelity has been at iffue with the eftablifhed religion of the country, thefe falutary effects have been fo few, as to be fcarcely perceptible.

Indeed, the majority of attendants upon thefe places, both of former, as well as recent date, have been led, by fucceffive gradations, to doubt of the very fundamentals before admitted! And he that began with fcruples, concerning fome parts of revelation, has commonly ended with queftioning the exiftence of a God! Thus Circe transformed men into beafts, but Atheifm converts them into monfters.

The fuppofition of a candid difcuffion in thefe affemblies is a mere farce; for in proportion as party-fpirit enlarges its fphere of action, candour is uniformly joftled out of its place. The number of hands held up, for or againft a queftion, is always more attended to, than the weight of the arguments

guments in its favour ; nor has any kind of ridicule been spared by the Infidels to ensure success over the Christians, when other means have proved abortive.

It has been intimated before, that the London Corresponding Society, by adding Deism to its politics, engendered the seeds of its own destruction : and, in fact, many of the leading orators, as if they were aware of going too far, after depreciating the character of the Saviour, in their harangues, used frequently to add the ridiculous assertion, " That they believed Jesus Christ was a " good republican." This mischievous levity, this superficial disposition, was carried into every scene of private, as well as public life. Having no taste but for scandal and declamation, among the multiplicity of publications which they sanctioned, no work upon the relative duties, no work inculcating moral or religious obligations to virtue, was either called for, or made its appearance. Volney's Law of Nature, or Catechism of Reason, published by Eaton, is the only exception to this charge : but as an unerring indication of Infidel propensities, in a hundred houses furnished with Paine's Age of Reason, the former was not once to be found ! Neither Plato, Socrates, nor Antoninus, though praised by Voltaire, had any charms for the turbulent disciples of Paine and Mirabaud : and hence the advice of a parent or master, for the want of some standing rule or authority, is generally weak and ineffectual ; a deficiency frequently increased by the difference of opinion between a man and his wife. The woman, we will suppose, even from habit, prefers seeing her children dressed, and at church, on a Sunday; but not to disoblige her *enlightened* husband, who has read the Age of Reason, this is a point she

gives

gives up; the children remain all the forenoon in their every day drefs, or ftray into the fields, where they contract vicious habits; and thus, all the obligations that refult from a place of public worfhip; the influence of a copious hiftory of ftriking examples, and the fanctity and authority of ages is loft and evaded. But if a difpofition for reading is in any degree indulged, the fublimity of the facred Scriptures is perhaps bartered for the effufions of fome fuperficial or political pamphleteer!

In fact, the whole fyftem of domeftic economy feems reverfed, by the introduction of deiftical notions. I have obferved, that the heads of many induftrious families, who, previous to their *illumination*, made it an indifpenfible duty to appear *abroad* decently dreffed on a Sunday, would afterwards not only remain the whole day in their working dreffes, to fhew their contempt of the *Chriftian Sabbath*, but fpend it *at home* in fottifhnefs and ftupidity. And yet Paine's Age of Reafon, Godwin's Political Juftice, &c. have remained upon their fhelves, and full in the fight of their poffeffors during the whole time! Others, who before, were honeft and frugal, have become knavifh and luxurious; and while their tables were covered with all the varieties of the feafon, could, without fcruple of confcience, defraud their poorer neighbours of their juft dues. In other inftances, felf-murder has put a period to thefe fatal deviations from order and decency. Thus the minds, even of adults, after foaring for a fhort period in the vacuity which they were taught to confider as an enlightened region, undetermined what object to alight upon, have funk at length into the muddy pools of vice; or having nothing more to hope for, embraced that dreary fcepticifm which cannot promife a fafe conduct through this temporary exiftence:

iftence; from hence, thefe unhappy fubjects have not unfrequently fallen into a fituation fo truly deplorable as to baffle every remedy, but have lived the aftonifhment of all who knew their wanderings, and died without regret!

Inftead then, of the Millennium, which modern Infidels had promifed themfelves from the number of their converts, what has been the confequence? Their public and private efforts have equally failed; and, laftly, a number of their members have left them fpontaneoufly, convinced that their notions upon matters of faith could never be attended with any wholefome effects; a mode of conduct, as I have before obferved, fimilar to that of many members of the once famed Robin Hood Society. Nor is there any thing which an Infidel ought to dread more than the reaction of his own principles upon himfelf, from his inferiors or his dependants: I have known a recent inftance of a fervant refufing to pay a juft debt to his mafter; and, in reply to his reproof for fuch conduct, he pleaded· his mafter's pre-inftructions! The latter it feems, had made him his companion to the Clubs, and had frequently told him, " There was no account to be taken hereafter of actions in this life."

There was another fpecies of inconfiftency, which materially checked the diffemination of Infidel opinions in private families; that is to fay, the propenfity of feveral individuals to attend places of Chriftian Worfhip, though in the conftant habit of declaiming againft them all! When fuch perfons were afked the reafon of this conduct, their anfwers generally were, that they went merely for amufement, or, that the Preachers making excellent moral difcourfes, they fuppofed no harm could be taken; a tacit confeffion of the weaknefs of their own fundamentals: but not refting here, this produced

duced a ſtrong propenſity in their children or ſer-
vants to doubt their ſincerity in other reſpeſts, and
frequently gave the whole of their objeſtions againſt
Chriſtianity the caſt and colour of prejudice. Now
theſe involuntary teſtimonies to the natural power
of religion upon the human mind, may be urged
ſo far as to prove, that while Deiſts and Atheiſts
are appealing to *Nature* for the juſtification of their
irreligious opinions, that ſame *Nature*, is confirming
the truth of the Chriſtian ſyſtem, by compelling them,
as it were, to ſanſtion certain aſts of divine worſhip, in ſpite of their opinions, and the ſyſtem they
profeſs

Naturam expellas furcâ, tamen uſque recurret.

Theſe charges I preſume, belong to that claſs of
faſts, which no ſophiſtry can remove ; but, as many
of them will neceſſarily appear new, not having
been urged by former writers againſt Deiſm, let it
be remembered, that Infidelity having never gained
ſo much ground before, among the common people,
the ſcope of obſervation was proportionately nar-
rowed : for, till the Age of Reaſon was adopted
by the political ſocieties in the metropolis, Deiſm,
to ſay nothing of Atheiſm, was rather the affair of
a few iſolated individuals, than, as it has been ſince
that period, the concern of a conſiderable part of the
community. Another inſtance of the weakneſs and
inferiority of modern infidelity is, that manifeſt want
of paſſive, or ſuffering, virtue, which ſeems to be a
natural reſult of the laxity of its principles. The
Infidels therefore, had they continued a riſing ſeſt,
could never have been formidable ; paſſive virtue,
in a civil or a religious body, being the ſame as
diſcipline in an army : wanting it, both would aſt
without energy, or be ſubjeſt to a ſpeedy diſſolu-
tion.

tion. How unlike, then, are thefe philofophers to the *Original* Quakers, whom they are fond of propofing as a model to other Chriftian denominations ! Thefe Quakers, raifed themfelves into confequence by cherifhing the virtue, in which their modern pane-gyrifts are moft deficient : the true ground of their increafe was a perfeverance, arifing from motives univerfally difcountenanced by Deifts and Atheifts, that is to fay, a hope of reward beyond the prefent life.

In all the recent declamations againft the Chriftian Religion, it is a principal charge that its minifters are the moft fordid and temporizing beings upon earth. But how ftands it with their accufers ? As far as facts can fpeak for themfelves, I anfwer, that, when their domeftic concerns, or fincerity in what they profefs, does, as occafion offers, demand any facrifice of *intereft ; principle* is generally given up in its room, with very little fcruple ; an affertion, which if neceffary, could be juftified by a number of inftances. Chriftianity, on the contrary, daily ex-hibits its nobler facrifices of a *prefent* for a *future* good ; a virtue arifing from a temper totally incom-patible with the Infidel fyftem, which admits of nothing beyond time and fenfe, and thus excludes the poffibility of exercifing this duty towards man ; and a due confidence in the Creator. Of the philo-fophers, it has been juftly faid ;

—————————" *Ils ont l'art de detruire,*
Mais ils n'élevent rien."

Proceeding upon thefe falfe principles, while modern Infidels have promifed themfelves happinefs and unanimity in their families, difcord has followed. Among others of this clafs, the man who has taught his children to avoid a place of worfhip, as a place
of

of infection, will neverthelefs fend them to Church, if education and an annual fuit (for which he could pay) are the conditions of their attendance; or rather than his new-born infant fhould lofe the prefent of a frock, the good graces of a godmother and a few goffips, he will fubmit to have it baptized, and ftill continue to upbraid Chriftians, as the moft abfurd and inconfiftent beings in the univerfe!

Another, if a place is to be obtained under government, has no objection to receive the Sacrament as a qualification; and thus it happens that modern Infidelity inftead of reforming, tends to increafe the number of hypocrites!

As a farther proof of their proftitution of confcientious rectitude, a recent inftance has occurred of the difappointment of a Benefit Society, in their wifh to exclude a member for boring them with Paine's Age of Reafon; and who, much to their aftonifhment, to obviate their complaints, did not refufe to take an oath before a magiftrate, and to profefs his belief of that Bible which it had been his conftant endeavour to difcredit!

From fuch temporizing conduct in parents and mafters of families, what muft be the inferences of the children? Will they regard the precepts which are continually at variance with the practice of thofe who recommend them? Certainly, whenever the Infidel attempts to realize his theories, he betrays the moft confirmed ignorance of human nature. A want of fympathy and commifferation is alfo a common failing with thefe pretenders, who have at the fame time fome theory or other, conftantly in their heads for leffening the evils in fociety—which defect may perhaps be imputed to the fyftem of fatalifm, pretty general among them. If an Infidel refufe to contribute to the neceffities of his brother, he may tell you he has no motive,
not

not being a *free agent ;* and in this cafe may laugh at any reply that can be made to his objection. To infift upon the fuperiority of the Chriftian Religion, which fuggefts fuch a variety of motives for repeated acts of humanity and benevolence, would be needlefs ; I fhall, however, ftate one inftance : a perfon, known as a profeffor of religion, being folicited to join with others for the relief of a third perfon, confined for a fmall debt, at firft ftarted feveral objections ; but, faid the folicitor, fuch a one, and fuch a one, have come forward, and can *you as a Chriftian* refufe to contribute ? This being an argument *ad hominem,* which he was unable to refift, he gave liberally. But as the *Book of Nature,* fo much boafted of by Deifts, is not fo exprefs upon this fubject as the *Book of Revelation,* fuch an appeal as I have juft cited, cannot be made to an Infidel.

As it muft be evident to every reflecting mind, that our hopes and fears are the ftrongeft motives of all our actions ; to expatiate here upon the difference between ancient and modern Deifm would be unneceffary. To thofe not verfed in the ancient Pagan fyftems, I fhall only obferve, that while *modern* Infidels are too wife to admit of any future rewards or punifhments, the *ancients* had their expiatory facrifices, purifications, retributions, and judgment after death. Thefe doctrines, inftead of deftroying every medium which could affect the heart, or fix the imagination, prefented and propagated an infinity of ideas and motives of confideration ; while the modern philofophy, urges and infifts upon nothing beyond a *bare probability !* A motive which is often too weak to operate upon difciplined and exalted minds, and confequently is not in the leaft degree qualified to arreft and fix the groffer and more perverted apprehenfions of the

profane

profane and vulgar ; even the Pagan Polytheifm,
was as much fuperior to the inanity of modern Infidelity, as Chriftianity is to both of thofe fyftems.

Thus we have had a fpecimen of philofophers,
without philofophy, and reformers, unreformed :
men, of whom, in the language of Jude, we may
more truly fay, " Thefe are clouds without water,
" carried about by the winds, wandering ftars,
" raging waves of the fea, murmurers and com-
" plainers fpeaking evil of dignities."

I fhould have obferved, when fpeaking of the
inferiority of modern Deifts and Atheifts to the
ancient Pagans, that the notions of the former
have a tendency to render every plan of education,
vague and uncertain. For, being anxious to fupprefs any idea their children may entertain of a
Being, or Beings, fuperior to men, they are neceffarily excluded from moft of the benefits which the
imagination derives from works of tafte and the
hiftory of antiquity. The *fyftem* of modern Infidelity, if fuch it may be called, has not the leaft
congeniality either with Polytheifm, or the Chriftian
Faith. Equally defpifing Heroes and Demi-Gods,
Saints and Angels ; Infidels can never be elevated
with exalted ideas of purity or fuperior excellence :
and of courfe, befides being deprived of the pleafure of wandering in the flowery fields of ufeful
and agreeable fiction, they may lofe all the motives
to virtue and piety, which mufic, painting, and
poetry, are well known to inculcate.

To every one of thefe degraded mortals, who
pride themfelves in being nothing more than mere
organizations of matter, this fine appeal of the
minftrel does moft forcibly apply,

Oh! how canft thou renounce the boundlefs ftore,
Of charms, which Nature to her vot'ry yields?

The

The warbling woodland, the furrounding fhore,
The pomp of groves, the garniture of fields;
　All that the genial ray of morning gilds,
　And all that echoes to the fong of ev'n,
　　All that the mountain's fheltring bofom fhelds,
　And all the dread magnificence of heaven,
Oh! how can'ft thou renounce and hope to be forgiven!
　　　　　　　　　　　　　　　BEATTIE.

Thus, all thefe low and obfcure puddles which I
have defcribed, flowing through fuch a variety ot
channels, have at length fettled in the ftagnant pool
of French Atheifm, which few have paffed in
fafety, where many have perifhed, and in which
many others may plunge, during the term of their
exiftence.

But even this, like the deadly lake of Sodom, has
its fruits, goodly to the eye, but mortal to the
tafte; and perhaps the fpecious appearance of
Atheiftic virtues was never more aptly illuftrated
than by the remark made, upon the French philofophers, by the late Emprefs of Ruffia. See Profeffor Robifon's Proofs of a Confpiracy, page 52,
53, 54. " *Ces philofophes*," faid fhe, " *font beaux,*
" *vus de loin; mais de plus pres le diamant parait*
" *chryftal:*" which may be rendered thus, " The
" actions and fentiments of thefe philofophers appear
" like *brilliants* at a diftance, but, clofely infpected,
" are nothing beyond *common pafte.*"

The natural inanity, froth, and vapour, of thefe
philofophical bodies, have appeared in various inftances, fince the period of their vifible decline;
the defection of a number of perfons, from the principles they profeffed, while in a collected ftate,
having proved, that they were only held together by
the vociferation of a few flippant leaders, ignorant
that *Religion is natural to civilized fociety.*

It has farther appeared, that many, even while
they remained with them, fo far from being con-
　　　　　　　　　　　　　　　　　　　　vinced

vinced by Infidel arguments, only wanted fome
perfon upon whofe judgment they could rely, to
bear them out in renouncing the whole, or the
principal parts of their new creed. And this recantation, it feems, was long declined by others,
left their *civifm* fhould be called in queftion ; *Deifm*
and *Democracy*, as it has been obferved before,
being deemed infeparable qualifications

Thus, as in France, fupported by external agency,
the meteor, which they falfely denominated, the
Light of Nature, might longer have continued to
aftonifh the multitude ; but even this admiration
muft have ceafed, when they found its rays afforded
no genial warmth ; that it led them into a tracklefs
void, and, after expofing them to all the ftorms of
adverfity in this life, left them without hope of re-
compenfe beyond the grave.

But, of the Chriftian fyftem it has been elegantly
faid,

> " Religion is a gen'rous lively flame,
> " That brightens, not deforms, the human frame :
> " A lambent light, around the heart it plies,
> " Not like a fury, threat'ning in the eyes.
> " No four reftraint, no forc'd concern it wears ;
> " No public fighs, no oftentatious tears ;
> " No felf-applauding boaft, no love of ftrife ;
> " No fpleen againft the blamelefs joys of life.
> " As far from thefe are Piety's fweet charms ;
> " As fettled courage from confus'd alarms ;
> " As folid Reafon's calm confiderate train,
> " From the wild frenzies of a moon-ftruck brain."

CHAP

CHAP. V.

Upon several recent Causes of Scandal upon the Established Religion.—Uncommon Increase of Itinerants.—Lady Ann's Preachers.—Visiting Preachers at Workhouses.—Societies for relieving the Poor at their own Habitations.—Character of the late Rev. Mr. Richards, Curate of St. Sepulchres.—Rev. R. Southgate.—Origin of the Swedenborgian Worship.—Popish Emigrants.

ONE of the principal evils, the subject of the present complaint, originates in the increasing and unprecedented number of preachers in what is called the Methodistic line, or at least, in the Calvinistic department of it, patronized by a Lady, the supposed successor, to the Countess of Huntingdon, and hence commonly called Lady Ann's preachers. This description, besides such of them as obtain appointments within doors, are generally to be found haranguing the passengers on a Sunday, during the summer-season, in the Spa-Fields, or in the avenues leading to Islington, Hackney, &c. most of them beardless boys, and mechanics or labourers by profession, whose ignorance of their mother-tongue is not to be equalled, since the business of out-door preaching was *lain* down by Oliver's preachers.

Many of the former, well known to persons acquainted with them before their metamorphosis, have contrived to appear out of doors, decorated in a gown, before they were well missed from their

in

ſhop-boards! What qualifications are deemed neceſſary to authorize ſo ſudden a change into a clerical habit I have never been able to learn, unleſs
volubility be miſtaken for elocution.

That ſeveral of theſe upſtarts were apprentices
at the time they commenced their miniſterial career,
particularly one of them, who fancied he was ſent
to call the Jews, (in Duke's Place) is a fact notori-
ouſly known. Hence the moſt nauſeating egotiſm,
and the want of every requiſite, except aſſurance,
are ſufficient to make religion itſelf (in the eyes of
the undiſcerning) acceſſary to its own diſgrace,
without the additional ridicule of Deiſts and Atheiſts, who are happy in the opportunities of charg-
ing the follies of a few upon the whole profeſſion.

Numbers of the ſame claſs, as to ability, have alſo
obtruded themſelves as miſſionaries to foreign parts.
One of theſe, now a carman to a tradeſman near
Smithfield, was abſolutely ſhipped for Sierra Leona,
ſoon after that colony was eſtabliſhed, but was
obliged to return in conſequence of a diſagreement with the natives.

Though not generally known, it is no leſs a
truth, that ſeveral of the workhouſes, in this metropolis, have been uſed as places of training and
exerciſe for, ſome years paſt, by theſe fanatical
adventurers.. Some of them, for what they term
exerciſing *their gifts*, abſolutely give the poor women in theſe houſes a few halfpence, on a Sunday,
to purchaſe ſnuff, tea, &c. which is again charged
to thoſe who employ the preachers, as a part of
their ordinary expences.

At ſome of the workhouſes, according to the
diſpoſition of the governors, the viſiting preachers
receive ſmall gratifications for their labours; for inſtance, a poor creature, now in the habit of attending Clerkenwell-workhouſe, generally receives a
ing

glafs of gin, as the reward of his vifit, and is farther allowed the privilege of trucking with his humble auditors for the houfe allowances of pudding,
cheefe, &c with which he fills his pockets, upon
his return home from what he calls his fermon!
This is the fame perfon mentioned in page 19, in the
double capacity of bird-catcher and field-preacher.

Till a regulation happily took place, a few years
fince, fome men of this charaċter ufed to force themfelves upon the malefaċtors under fentence of death.
In conformity with the complaint, here advanced, it
has been the opinion of feveral judicious obferv-
ers of the manners and morals of mankind, " that
" great hurt has been done by the fanatical conver-
" fation, the vifionary hymns, and the bold and im-
" pious applications of the Scriptures, by fuch
" people above defcribed, when attending con-
" demned malefaċtors. It cannot be denied that,
" in confequence of the moft culpable proftitution
" of facred things, many daring offenders againft
" law and juftice have had their paffions and ima-
" ginations fo worked upon, and have been fent into
" the other world in fuch raptures, as would much
" better become martyrs, innocently fuffering in a
" glorious caufe, than criminals of the firft mag-
" nitude." In fine, the conduċt of thefe *immoral*
preachers of *religion* appeared in fo odious a light,
a few years fince, that it induced the magiftrates
of the city of London to confine the office of attending upon the prifoners in general to the Ordinary of Newgate; but, being refufed there, I can
fee no reafon they fhould gain admittance into
the workhoufes.

A poem, called the Literary Cenfus, which I
have before me, thus defcribes fome of the cha-
raċters, who are the conftant means of heaping
fcandal upon the eftablifhed religion.

" In

" In terms uncouth, and myftic phrafe they rave
" Of faving faith and faith that cannot fave,
" The fpirit's teaching, and the fpirit's rod,
" And how the Devil over-reaches God ;
" How lion-like he feeketh to devour,
" And damns more fouls than grace to fave has pow'r.
" You'd fwear, fo loud their rant, and fo abftrufe,
" Bedlam, or Babel's workmen, were let loofe."

In a note to page 88 of this pamphlet, I find
the opinion of this ingenious author, upon the mul-
tiplication of thefe fanatical fchifmatics, exactly
fimilar to the impreffions I had previoufly entertained, from a confideration of their conduct ; I
have therefore taken the liberty of tranfcribing it
at full length.

" The incalculably rapid increafe of thefe lo-
" cufts, and the obloquy their frantic demeanor,
" ignorance, and vulgarity, entail upon true reli-
" gion, and the refpectable part of the clergy,
" render the interference of the legiflature indif-
" penfably neceffary. If any of the magiftrates
" of the realm fhould honour this work with a
" perufal, they will acknowledge that my remarks
" are juft. Mr. Mainwaring, to his credit, has
" exerted himfelf, as far as the power vefted in him
" by law will permit, to fupprefs this unfufferable
" nuifance ; but, as the law ftands at prefent, the
" hands of magiftrates are tied, and they fcarcely
" dare refufe a licence to the moft contemptible
" blockhead, who believes, or wifhes to make
" others believe, he has received a call. I am
" credibly informed, and I honour the gentleman
" for his conduct on the occafion, that the magif-
" trate whom I above named experienced fome
" difficulty in rejecting the application of a mean
" defpicable wretch, who, upon being queftioned
" what profeffion he followed, proved to be a *bellows-
blower

" *blower to a forge*, and was so shockingly illiterate,
" that he could not even tell the letters of the
" alphabet. The subjoined list, of some of the
" recently-ordained retailers of the Gospel, was
" communicated to me, by a worthy and religious
" friend, and will serve to illustrate the propriety
" of the preceding remarks:

Mr. Norton,	Dealer in Old Clothes,
Mr. Wilson,	Grinder,
Mr. Timothy Hinds,	Sheeps-Head Seller,
Mr. Saunders,	Coach-Painter,
Mr. Colston,	Pressman,
Mr. O———,	Mangle-Maker,
Mr. Downes,	Glazier,
Mr. Hickup,	Footman to J. G. Esq.
Mr. Staunton,	Tooth-Drawer, Peruke-Maker, and Phleboto-mist,
Mr. Parry,	Breeches-Maker, &c. &c.

" Almost, *ad infinitum;* not less than 397 having
" taken out Preaching-Licences, at the New
" Sessions-House, Clerkenwell, in the course of
" the years 1796-7."

The author goes on to observe, " That, having
" once touched upon this subject, it would be
" an act of injustice to dismiss it, without observing,
" as it accounts, in a great degree, for the vast
" number of upstart teachers and doctrines for
" which this country is pre-eminently distinguish-
" ed, that, there is, in this metropolis, a *ci-devant*
" Coal-heaver, notorious for no qualification upon
" earth, but consummate impudence and incor-
" rigible ignorance, whom, I am given to under-
" stand, is in the receipt of nearly £1000 *per*
" *annum*. He is proprietor and *fac totum* of two
" chapels,

" chapels, and has lately purchafed the elegant
" manfion of the late Dr. M——h, with grounds
" and appurtenances; in addition to which, he
" keeps his carriage."

Two months after I had determined upon fketch-
ing out an account of the fcandals occafioned to
religion, by illiterate enthufiafts; and, after I had
proceeded thus far in the execution of my defign, I
learned, with pleafure, that this fubject of complaint had been noticed in the Houfe of Commons: on Monday, Februry 3, M. Angelo Taylor
gave notice of an intended motion; and in which,
he afked relief in the cafe of licenfing preachers;
urging, that, within a very fhort time, he had
been applied to, and obliged to grant a licence
to a boy of feventeen years of age, as a *Preacher
of the Gofpel!*

I may now add, fince writing the laft remark,
the additional fatisfaction of finding my obfervations, upon the wretched ignorance of thefe
itinerant preachers, fully confirmed by the Report from the Clergy of the Diocefe of Lincoln,
convened, the firft time in Auguft laft, for the
purpofe of confidering the State of Religion;
Printed for Rivington, St. Paul's Church-yard,
and Hatchard, Piccadilly.

In this valuable production, one of the leading
caufes of the dangers arifing to the church and
government of this kingdom, and the alarming
increafe of profanenefs and irreligion, is juftly
imputed to thofe Methodifts, fuch as I have defcribed in London, " who attend and encourage
" a wandering tribe of fanatical teachers, moftly
" taken from the loweft and moft illiterate claffes
" of fociety; among whom are to be found, ra-
" ving enthufiafts, pretending to divine impulfes,
" of various and extraordinary kinds, practifing
                                    " exorcifms,

" exorcifms, and many other forts of impoftures
" and delufions, and obtaining, thereby, an un-
" limited fway over the minds of the ignorant
" multitude."

This third and loweft clafs of perfons, to
whom the name of Methodifts is ufually given,
it is alfo obferved, are neither qualified by education for the office of teachers, nor bound by
the declaration of any fixed principles, nor re-
ftrained by any fenfe of decency or fhame; and
fo various are their abfurdities, that they feem
to have no point of union, except a determination to calumniate the eftablifhed Clergy, which
defign they execute with unrelenting violence and
malice, at all times, and in all places. " Some
" of them, it is repeated, practife exorcifms, and
" capricious forms, and modes of it, utterly in-
" confiftent, not only with religious gravity but
" with morality and decency: they have alfo
" frequently denounced the reprobation not only
" of particular perfons and families but of whole
" villages, and publicly execrated the churches,
" as being nothing but a heap of ftones."

This report, evidently dictated by a fpirit of
moderation and veracity, farther imputes " the
" propagation of thefe mifreprefentations and im-
" impoftures to the private affemblies, known by
" the name of Claffed Meetings;" but it does
not dwell upon the unprecedented influence of
the leaders of thefe *bands*, as they are called.
The latter are, to all intents and purpofes, Father-
Confeffors, in their way; and though generally lefs
informed than the preachers, to which office they
occafionally afcend, yet thefe men are profeffion-
ally called upon, to hear the fecrets of families,
and to determine upon, and direct fuch intricate
movements of the mind as would juftly require
the

the fkill of an acute philofopher, or a judicious divine; but, being filled by illiterate zealots, their manner of queftioning young perfons, relative to their fenfations arifing from attachments, &c. &c. has not feldom been the fubjeƈt of obfervation and cenfure.

More information refpeƈting the extraordinary miffions of Lay Methodift-preachers, in the country, may be copioufly colleƈted from the Evangelical and other Magazines, ftill in circulation, under the head of Religious, or Miffionary Intelligence. Perhaps thefe are neither of the loweft nor the moft mifchievous defcription; however, all muft tend to fhew, that, " the interefting ftatement of faƈts " contained in the Report of the Diocefe of Lincoln is " really applicable to a great part of " the kingdom," and that the complaint ferioufly calls for the attention of the Legiflature, by the inlet which it gives to Socinianifm, Deifm, and even Atheifm. And, farther, that, " the fame means " might, with equal efficacy, be employed to fap " and overturn the ftate, as well as the church; " of which fome flagrant inftances have not been " wanting."

If the fame fcrutiny, thus happily begun in the Diocefe of Lincoln, fhould be applied in London, we fhall then find the fame defigns of thefe low and bigotted Seƈtarifts branched out into a thoufand fhapes. One of their methods, not generally known, and in which fome of the moft illiterate bear a principal part, is, in qualifying themfelves for a more public miniftry, by vifiting the fick-poor at their own houfes; being employed, by various focieties, rather with a view of making profelytes than to alleviate, as they profefs, the temporal wants of the indigent and fick: for, if the perfons vifited hear their exhortations with patience,

half-

half-a-crown is the utmoſt reward of their attention; and the viſits and the donation may be repeated twice or thrice. But if, on the contrary,
no diſpoſition is ſhewn to adopt the *particular
mode of faith*, profeſſed by theſe humble Miſſionaries, (I ſpeak from certain knowledge) inſtances
have not been wanting, when they have departed
without leaving any evidences of their *charity!*

Now, while, by the operation of theſe proſelyting
agents, falſe religion is palmed upon the unwary
for the true; and, while the mere endeavour to
increaſe a party borrows the name of piety, it is
evident, that a conſtant ſource of ſcandal, againſt
the eſtabliſhed church, is kept open, and daily
adding to thoſe uncharitable diviſions, of which
Infidels are ever ready to avail themſelves, for depreciating religion in general.

It is much to be lamented, that ſo many opportunities preſent themſelves to theſe fanatics;
it is, perhaps, one of the incurable evils attendant
upon a numerous population. However, that
much might be done to counteract them, even
in the metropolis, is clear, from what has been
done already. The memory of the Rev. Mr.
Richards, Curate of St. Sepulchre's in this city,
is ſtill freſh in the minds of his pariſhioners: his
diligence, during thirty years reſidence, in viſiting,
relieving, and admoniſhing, the lower orders of
people, both within and beyond the bounds of his
pariſh, has made an impreſſion on the minds of all
that knew him which will never be effaced.
Unbleſſed with any brilliancy of parts, or a captivating addreſs, his ſteady and indefatigable per-
ſeverance, in the line of his duty, alone enſured
him that fame, which he never ſought after.

Though truly humble in his deportment, ſo far
from expoſing him to inſult, his conduct and appearance

pearance would frequently call forth the warmeſt wiſhes for his welfare, as he paſſed through the ſtreets. He was, indeed, gentle and eaſy to be intreated, and was frequently known to riſe from his table, to attend any ſudden call for his ſervices. He died ſo truly lamented, that, as many perſons can teſtify, there were very few dry eyes at the period of his interment in his own pariſh-church.

But, with very little income beſides his curacy, it is not to be ſuppoſed the many that partook of his bounty owed their obligations to him alone. As I am informed, ſeveral well-diſpoſed perſons, convinced of his integrity, depoſited their alms with him, to be diſtributed at his diſcretion: an office which he had the faculty of executing without letting the receivers feel their inferiority, though it was never unaccompanied by ſome ſuitable admonition. A Reverend Gentleman, in giving evidence upon the trial of Jane Gibbs, at the Old Bailey Seſſions, for September, 1799, mentioned his own precaution of wearing an *unpowdered wig, becauſe Clergymen could not paſs along the ſtreets without being inſulted.* A moſt ſurpriſing aſſertion! for though the late truly-pious Curate of St. Sepulchre's uſed to be remarkable for a plainneſs of dreſs, almoſt bordering upon meanneſs, and wore a white buſhy wig, the populace were ſo far from inſulting him, that even the butchers in Fleet-market, and the very loweſt and profligate charaĉters in the pariſh, have borne his admonitions with temper and reſpeĉt; and this, in the moments of exceſs. Severe examples, no doubt, would have been made of any perſon attempting to have treſpaſſed againſt this truly good man, beyond the bounds of decency or good manners; an inſtance of which, was never known to have occurred.

But

But independently of the influence of perfonal virtue, the populace of this city has never degenerated fo low, as to juftify the unheard-of precaution of Dr Ford, which, if well founded, would have given fuch of our Gallic neighbours, as have thrown off the Chriftian religion, an idea, that we were in a very hopeful way. The contrary, I believe, thoufands as well as myfelf are ready to teftify.

It fhould have been mentioned, that Mr. Richards, having no children, though married, took one of the girls out of a large family belonging to one of his parifhioners ; not to bring her up as a menial fervant, as might have been expected, but whom he caufed to be educated as one of his own ; and, after his deceafe, fhe was the companion of his pious relict, his conftant imitator in acts of piety and condefcenfion.

But befides the public and private duties of his own parifh, Mr. Richards, for a confiderable time, was engaged in the painful and difcouraging tafk of officiating at Clerkenwell-Bridewell. Here, his admonitions in the pulpit were always feconded by acts of kindnefs to fuch prifoners as fhewed any figns of contrition and amendment ; a ftamp of fincerity and condefcenfion on his part, which was very feldom loft upon the objects with whom he was engaged.

The late Rev. Mr. Richard Southgate, of St. Giles's in the Fields, was another of thefe valuable characters. He was, fays one of his biographers, " in the daily habit of vifiting the retreats of fick- " nefs and mifery, and the moft abandoned and " profligate in the holes and corners of that parifh." And yet, like Mr. Richards's parifhioners, they treated him with that good manners which they paid no one elfe. It fhould be obferved, that
the

the pooreſt of the Iriſh, who form a principal part of Mr. Southgate's late pariſh, though Catholics, treat a regular Clergyman with conſiderable reſpeĉt.

Before ſuch conduĉt as this, how wretched a figure muſt the Infidel maxim make, " That every " prieſt is either a knave or a fool." A conduĉt which muſt for ever ſilence the objeĉtions both of Infidels and fanatics, by demonſtrating, in the ſtrongeſt manner, that a paſtor of an exemplary life, is " *an incalculable bleſſing.*" Perhaps, with others, who have borne the appellation of evangelical preachers, the late Rev Mr. Berridge was a paſtor, juſtly eſteemed a bleſſing to his people.

The real friend and companion of his pariſhioners in the country, Mr. Berridge's charity and officious attention was the moſt impreſſive recommendation of the doĉtrine which he delivered from the pulpit. In faĉt, one would think the bare recolleĉtion of the natural and acquired abilities of ſuch miniſters as Meſſrs. Berridge, Percy, Peckwell, &c. would force a bluſh for the compariſon betwèen them and Lady Ann's preachers ; but, for the credit of the cauſe, this Lady would be thought to ſupport, it is hoped that, in future, ſome education will be a *firſt* and not a SECONDARY conſideration for theſe young men, at preſent decorated as ſcholars, while, inſtead of being apt to teach ; their friends pity, and their enemies deride them : ſo that the injunĉtion once delivered to ſome others, *viz.* " to tarry at Jeruſalem till their beards were grown," ſeems particularly applicable to their ſtate and condition.

Innovations, in matters of faith, always weaken the obligations of religion, and ſometimes ſcandalize its profeſſors ; of courſe, the opinions of Baron Sweden-

Swedenborg, approaching nearer than any others to modern Infidelity, may be suppofed to have adminiftered in proportion to the objections of Deifts and Atheifts. What muft thefe think of a fect, who, under the appellation of Chriftians, explain away the doctrine of the atonement, the refurrection, and the day of judgment? Let them be told, that, from the canon of the New Teftament, this new fect have excluded all the Epiftles, which they clafs as *private letters!* That with them the day of judgment is more a *figure* than a *fact:* that it commenced about 1758, in the printing and publication of the judgment of Emmanuel Swedenborg, to condemn, collectively, all the doctrines of the *Old*, or Trinitarian, church.

Thefe and feveral other opinions, held by the difciples of the New church, would certainly meet much of the approbation of Infidels, as fome of the moft eligible means of bringing Chriftianity in general into difrepute.

The principal article of this felf-called *New* church, it fhould be obferved, is juft as *Old* as Muggleton and Reeves; who, after the protectorfhip of Oliver, were the firft who publifhed, that the whole godhead is circumfcribed in the perfon of Jefus Chrift, ftill retaining the human form. in heaven; the *belief of which*, and not *repentance*, both Muggletonians and Swedenborgians enforce upon their followers, as the *firft* and moft effential condition of gofpel acceptance.

Notwithftanding all the recommendation of a pompous worfhip among the new fect of Swedenborgians, the fantaftical difpofal of the two officiating minifters in one chapel, and the drefs of the paftor in another, imitating a *Chef de Famille*, among the French theophilanthropifts, a new liturgy, and the fubftitution of the name of the

temple

temple for that of church, so slow is their progress in making proselytes, that to prepare for a decent retreat, some of their leaders have published an opinion, that it never was the design of the illuminated Baron, to found any new mode of public worship upon his doctrines.

But notwithstanding this hint, and a previous failure at the West end of the town, another temple has been opened in York-street, St. James's, namely, the late Roman Catholic chapel; into which, if some persons should enter, while the minister (according to a former custom in the temple, near Hatton-Garden) is reading with his back towards the congregation, the place may still be taken for what it has been, and tend to confirm the vulgar opinion of a resemblance between this *New* church, and the *Old* church of Rome.

Having failed of success in the Eastern part of the metropolis, which abounds with religious persuasions of all denominations, mechanics, and others, with less learning and leisure to make inquiries, than the inhabitants of the Court end of the town, it requires no gift of prophecy to predict the fate of the New church in York-street, St James's. As for the apology, that it never was the will of the Baron to establish a new form of worship, after a series of unsuccessful attempts for twelve years past, it is nothing more than a clumsy attempt to make a virtue of necessity. The real cause of this preparation, for a decent exit, is in the doctrines themselves, which have too much of the metaphysics for the head, and too little energy for the heart; and of course are not adapted to obtain any lasting interest with the generality of men, after their novelty has subsided. Nor can they produce that change upon the profligate, which succeeds to stronger motives, congenial with the natural ideas which uncontami-

nated

nated judgments entertain of the refults of virtue and vice: a change, which notwithftanding always follows a cordial belief of the doctrines generally taught by the *Old Church* of England; but which the *New* and *enlightened Church*, is led to confider as " a tiffue of fhocking abfurdities."

As the origin of Swedenborgianifm in this country differs from that of any other religion that 1 know of, a little farther digreffion may be excufed. In moft cafes, new fects have been collected by the fuperior addrefs or elocution of the original founders. Thus, in the inftance of Methodifm, the powerful appeals made to the minds of numbers of people, grounded upon the doctrines of the Church of England, did really excite and perfuade great bodies of them to adopt its principles, feeling their mental intereft in fo doing. Not fo, the founders of Swedenborgianifm, a fect, which literally originated in a printer's job! being hatched in the parifh of Clerkenwell, near the fpot where the Baron had his obfcure lodging, *viz.* at a hair-dreffer's, in Bath-ftreet, Cold-Bath-Fields, while he refided in this country. Its next appearance was in an alley. in Little Eaftcheap, partly in the modern and fafhionable form of a debating fociety: but, inftead of preachers collecting the people, thefe people were fo hard run to collect preachers, that for a confiderable time the office was generally confined to the printer alluded to, and one of his relatives. After fome of the Baron's works were tranflated, and publifhed in this city, the idea of quickening a heavy fale might have had its weight in the attempts to make them the bafis of a new mode of worfhip. The celebrity of the Baron was, in the next place, diffufed by the publication of the Magazine of Heaven and Hell; and a Romance, calculated to introduce

troduce his, or rather the principles of his editor's, among the ladies; fo that with the fubfequent labours of fome ingenious men, and the affiftance of a few of the wealthy, in opening Temples at Manchefter, Birmingham, &c. they have hitherto contrived to keep the name of the fect alive, notwithftanding fome fteps have been taken for withdrawing altogether from any farther exhibition in public. Yet, if appearances are to be trufted, the moft heterodox opinions that ever bore the name of Chriftianity, will not trouble the orthodox much longer.

This pageant, this pantomime of religion, having no fund of fupport, but a flender annuity in the lives of a few wealthy individuals, can never defcend to pofterity, nor exift but as an additional article in the catalogue of fome Alexander Rofs's Hiftory of All Religions. From appearances, one would fuppofe this fect already verging towards bankruptcy, as it is not long fince a fubfcription was opened to reprint the works of the Baron, in which the fmall fum of one penny a week was not unacceptable.

How are the mighty fallen!

The late difpofition for a more extenfive fufferance of the Roman Catholic religion, and efpecially the relief of the unfortunate Emigrant Clergy, has not only been the fubject of bitter invective in the clubs, but out of them, fome zealots, bearing the Chriftian name, have gone fo far as to publifh heavy cenfures upon the late Rev. W. Romaine, merely for collecting alms for the Emigrants. People of this caft, and thofe profeffing Infidelity, wifhed to fee all the ancient animofities between Proteftant and Papift, revived in the prefent war. To inflame the Proteftants againft a government that entered into an alliance with Popifh powers; and, laftly, with the Pope himfelf, was a favourite undertaking;

dertaking; but here, exclusively of political motives, these calumniators, were not aware, that their own partizans in irreligion, the French Robesperians, by proclaiming death an eternal sleep, and other enormities, had left their opponents no medium to choose between Atheism, and the old established religion of the country. The new philosophy then, by its unqualified opposition to the Catholic religion, was the indirect cause of all the protection, the latter has since met with from the enemies of the republic.

Glad, indeed, would have been the partizans of Atheism, could they have persuaded Dissenters, and others, that the Protestant religion was really in danger. But, unhappily for them, while they were spreading alarms of the growth of Popery, some of its chapels in the metropolis, were actually shut up, for want of their usual support from abroad. And thus, from the charity of the English Clergy towards the Emigrants, the enemies of both were reduced to the necessity of branding an exemplary virtue with the character of a vice!

In concluding this narrative, I have the conscious satisfaction, that I have removed none of the ancient landmarks between things sacred and profane; that I have administered to no new sect or division; and that my design, however weakly executed, has not been to destroy, but to build up; to strengthen the weak, and confirm the feeble. But did sectarians, who build speculative opinions, even upon the ancient foundations, previously reflect, they could have little hope of benefiting mankind. If they fail in their attempts, they only reap shame and remorse; and, if they succeed, it is probable, that they lay the foundation of new feuds and dissentions; and, like the madman mentioned in the Proverbs, " scatter firebrands, arrows, and death."

Having

Having now gone through a detail of all the late branches of modern Infidelity, without the leaft known deviation from matter of fact; and having fhewn that the focieties owed their diffolution principally to the reaction of their own maxims and opinions, I fhall now leave the application of thefe facts to the country at large.

But, as there are numbers, who ftill indulge the ruinous fentiments of Deifm and Atheifm, and only wait for an opportunity of rallying their fcattered forces, I fhall now offer a few more reflexions upon the operation of thofe fentiments; not merely as they have hitherto been argued from, in books; but as they have occurred in real life, fince the habit of difbelieving the Chriftian religion has been fafhionable. In thefe reflections I flatter myfelf that I fhall demonftrate the blindnefs of Infidels, in perfifting to fhut their eyes againft the cleareft convictions of truth and reafon.

GENERAL CONSIDERATIONS.

On the Influence of Infidel Opinions upon Society; anfwering the various Objections of Modern Deifts and Atheifts againft the Doctrines of Chriftianity.

Non leve momentum apud nos habet confenfus omnium, aut timentium inferos, aut colentium.

SENECA.

THERE is, undoubtedly, a fecret caufe, why the moft convincing arguments, hitherto urged againft *modern* Deifm and Atheifm, have failed of effect, *viz.* a general perfuafion among the *illuminated*, the *new* pretenders to *philofophy*, " that, under " fome fyftem of government more favourable " than the prefent, their doctrines will certainly " difplay their fuperiority, in exterminating thefe " vices and *individual calamities*, which, during the " prefent order of things, muft remain as they are."

Now, without waiting for this imaginary period, the beft mode of inveftigating the folidity of this affertion, will be to examine what progrefs has been made in this fuppofed fcale of perfection.

As

As Infidels have a natural antipathy to miracles, they will the more readily admit, that every fpecies of reformation has its gradations; the progrefs, therefore, that you have already made upon a part of the community, is the beft criterion to enable us to judge of your probable fuccefs upon the whole.

To come to matter of fact: During the five years in which the diffemination of your opinions has been comparatively free, Have any of you been able to convince the whole circle of your acquaint-ance, a whole houfe, or a whole family, of the fal-fity or irrationality of the Chriftian doctrines?

If to thefe interrogations you are compelled to anfwer, No; Where then is the probability of your fucceeding upon a larger fcale?

The Roman fatyrift, Juvenal, has obferved, that a fingle houfe will fhew whatever is done or fuffered in the world; it then follows that, if the little Theatre, upon which you have acted, had been en-larged, it would only have expofed you fo much the more, to the hiffes and infults of a difappointed audience. In fact, the recent fhutting up of the great Theophilanthropic Theatre in Paris, though fupported by all the ftrength of the Republican go-vernment, is a convincing proof, that no inferior attempt will ever fucceed, efpecially in a country, which, in oppofition to the comparative levity of the French, has borne the proud diftinction of " A " nation of philofophers."

Deftitute of every kind of public worfhip, beyond a mere fête or fhew, I would afk you, what im-preffion this is likely to make upon fullen and un-toward difpofitions? Levelling all diftinctions be-tween facred and profane, you, alas! have no hiftory either to feize the imagination, or intereft the paf-fions. But, without this, be your public inftitutions

or

or your Religious Fêtes ever fo fplendid, ftill, as
Pliny faid of the Circean games ; *Nihil novum, nihil
varium, nihil quod non femel fpectaffe fufficiat,* muft
ever apply to fuch exhibitions. Not fo, either the
doctrines or dogmas of the Chriftian Religion, they
are fuited to every neceffity, and adapted to every
difpofition. Even the diverfity and variety of fenfes,
attached to the different parts of the facred Scriptures, are the ground of unanimity upon general
principles ; they fix the attention, they excite the
difcurfive faculties in the mind, or they elevate or
fuftain it under adverfity ; while the cold and un-
diverfified fymmetry, which your fyftem of *reafon*
would fuggeft, grows wearifome by its famenefs,
and difgufting from its uniformity. Indeed, while
you muft acknowledge, that the " paffions are the
elements of life," your introduction of a fyftem,
which tends to quench, or deftroy them, is one of
the moft glaring of inconfiftencies.

We, you fay, only wifh to cultivate and improve
the faculty of reafon ; this leads to the charge of
another abfurdity and inconfiftency in your conduct
as philofophers, which I fhall immediately confider.
Is it poffible that the cultivation of reafon fhould
be your principal object, while you are actually
deftroying or undermining the ftrongeft incitements
to the exercife of the reafoning powers? I am
aware, that in confequence of your prejudices, you
will not readily comprehend this charge ; but I will
explain myfelf. The great truths of Religion, which
fix and recall the wandering fenfes and affections of
men, you endeavour to refolve into vain fears and
ufelefs chimeras. Thofe fentiments, which power-
fully ftimulate the mind to a calculation of the probable effects of moral good or evil, you deride as
folly and enthufiafm ! You muft know that a vola-
tility and inconftancy of mind is common to youth ;

and

and that it is indifpenfably neceffary to fix this vo-
latility, before the faculty of laying down premifes,
and reafoning from conclufions, can be introduced.
You fhould know alfo, that the attachment of pains
and penalties to the non-performance of thefe conditions is neceffary to excite men to aftion : but inftead of the ftrong motives of everlafting happinefs
and mifery, as they are expreffed in the Scriptures,
what are the inducements of your code ? The *Reafon and Fitnefs of Things !* the perfuafion that
virtue is its own reward; that human aftions are neceffary ; that man is accountable to man only for
any of his aftions ! As thefe are charges which you
can neither palliate nor deny, will you have the
effrontery to affert, that the laxity and indifference
attending thefe notions have not an indireft tendency to annihilate the neceffity of reafon or calculation ? Men who cannot be interefted in your creeds,
beyond giving them a bare affent, can never fuppofe themfelves under the neceffity, either to compare or judge of the probabilities, or improbabilities
of any other fyftem ; and principally becaufe, beyond the opinion of the world, they have no ftake
to hazard.

On the other hand, the Chriftian, however mean
his natural abilities may be ; however weak and
unpraftifed his reafoning faculties, if once roufed
from his vices, or fupinenefs, by the awakening voice
of Religion, it is more than a hundred to one, if
his reafoning powers are not much improved by the
change. It then becomes his irrefiftible intereft to
reafon upon the confequences of emerging from, or
apoftatizing into, the ftate from which he had been
awakened. In faft, he not only becomes a Na-
turalift, but he may exalt his faculties ftill higher, by
contemplating the nature and attributes of Deity,
or thofe intelligences fuperior to man : a fphere to
which

which the poor alienated Infidel has no excitement. The Chriftian, in the former ftate, like the prodigal fon reftored to the houfe of his father, truly enjoys an intellectual feaft; while the Infidel, a fugitive, and an outcaft, and efpecially, if he be a fenfualift, may be faid to *feed upon the hufks with the fwine.* Deluded men! and is this the ftate of degradation for which you plead? Reafon, you affert, is the great object for which you contend; and yet, rejecting the doctrine which can beft allay and tranquillize the impetuous paffions, and forfaking that calm region where its voice can only be heard, you deftroy the means by which you fhould arrive at the end propofed! That many of you are not reafoners, at leaft from your own principles, cannot be denied. But what was the primeval caufe of this exertion? Moft of your leaders, originally profeffing the Chriftian Religion, are indebted to its faith and doctrines, for the *primum mobile,* which gave the firft impulfe to their rational faculties; firft excited and fharpened the talent of inveftigation : nor would they have been able to wound Religion, if they had not firft ftolen her arrows.

Perhaps, the thunders of that religion, you now deride, were the means of arrefting fome of you in a courfe of fenfuality, which would ultimately have fmothered every latent fpark of ratiocination then dormant in your minds ; and does it thus become *you* to depreciate the only medium, by which you have rifen to your recent diftinction? Still, this abfurdity, peculiar to modern Infidelity, does not reft here ; for degenerating into downright ingratitude, like an offspring perfectly unnatural, you chiefly fuftain your character by defcanting upon the vices or frailties of the parent ftock; beyond the fphere of declamation, you cannot exift. The *reformation* you pretend to advocate, would be your *ruin.*
Like

Like the animalculæ, bred upon the filth of creation, you delight in clinging to the weak fide of humanity. You have no fuftenance which you do not derive from its wounds No foundation which is not built upon the ruin of others. Your confequence is enhanced by their degradation; and your unanimity derives all its force from the divifions, you are the firft to create or extend. Thefe charges, harfh as they may appear, I am not difpofed to fix in the malignity of your nature, but rather, in an over-weening vanity and affectation of knowledge. But as this mania has almoft exclufively taken poffeffion of young minds, it may behove you to reflect upon the influence thefe fceptical opinions may have in future upon your own happinefs, as fathers, hufbands, and other relatives. Ceafe, then, to boaft of perplexing a few weak minds by a hackneyed ftring of common place arguments, or drawing a multitude, by the torrent of your declamation : the majority of your objections to the Chriftian doctrines, as it will prefently appear, are grounded upon prejudice, and the want of a proper difcrimination.

First, I obferve, that what are called the atrocious **cruelties** of the Bible Hiftory, are in the mouth of every objector who has read Paine's Age of Reafon, without perufing the Anfwer of the Bifhop of Llandaff. But even granting the full force of the Infidel's objections, without infilting upon the purity of circumftances in God's government of the natural world, fo judicioufly urged by the learned Bifhop, I would fain know, what influence thefe hiftories of cruelty have upon the generality of Chriftians ? The acts complained of, were moftly perpetrated by Princes ; from whence there is little danger of their examples upon the people ; upon the fcore of inability : and befides, thefe acts are

placed

placed at fuch a diftant period, and are neceffarily involved in fuch a peculiarity of circumftances, as to produce very little, if any effect, upon the manners of civil fociety.

If the Infidel will ftill urge, that this inefficacy of example is equally applicable to the acts of piety and benevolence recorded in the Scriptures, I anfwer, that upon the latter, the minds of men are fond of dwelling with complacency and delight, and will frequently revolve them in their recollection ; while deeds of comparative atrocity are paffed over with indifference, and feldom, or ever made the fubject of meditation, nor even recurred to, without neceffity; or, in the courfe of their reading or worfhip. To prove the charge brought by Infidels, it is incumbent upon them to fhew that thofe denominations of Chriftians, who have drank the deepeft of Scripture knowledge, have perpetrated the greateft proportion of barbarities. Unhappily for Deifts and Atheifts, the contrary has been the fact, as the Papifts, to whom the reading of the Scriptures has been the moft part prohibited, have been almoft exclufively the perpetrators of the enormities, uncandidly charged upon Chriftians in general.

The natural cruelty of the Mahometans, is another argument in favour of the humanity of the Chriftian fyftem; notwithftanding the opinion of Infidels, that the former approach the neareft of the two, to the ftandard of reafon.

But, religious perfecution, though not peculiar to the Chriftian Religion, attaches to bigots of every defcription ; confequently it is an imputation, from which *unbelievers* are by no means free. Helvetius, one of the moft eminent of the modern materialifts, obferves, " there are few men who would " not employ violence to engage the world to adopt
" their

" their fentiments, if they had it in their power."
A ftronger truifm than this could not have been pronounced, had Helvetius been an eye-witnefs to all
the petty malignities made ufe of by his fucceffors
to the prefent day. Very little experience, among
this kind of people, is quite fufficient to fhew, that
a perfecuting fpirit is not peculiar to the Chriftian
communities.

Modern Infidels frequently calumniate our religion, in oppofing the forbearance of Pagans to
what they call, the perfecuting fpirit of the Chriftians ; a vice from which they fay, the former were
quite exempt. But to undeceive fuch perfons, I
fhall prefent them with the following inftances of
the contrary of their affertions, felected by a recent
writer in favour of Chriftianity.

Afpafia, having been accufed of impiety, owed
her father's life to the interceffion of Pericles, and
the tears he fhed while pleading her caufe.

Anaxagoras, of Clafomenæ, was in danger of
lofing his head, for afferting that the fun was a
huge mafs of hot iron.

Diagoras, of Melos, had a talent fet upon his
head, for ridiculing the religious myfteries.

Protagoras, having queftioned the exiftence of
the gods, only efcaped death by flight.

And, laftly, Socrates was compelled to drink
poifon at Athens, by an exprefs law of that city,
againft any perfon who fhould be the introducer of
a new god.

But leaving the ancients to inquire, whether
modern Infidels would not be as violent perfecu-
tors as any others whom they accufe, and even
greater than Chriftians have been ; this, I prefume,
may be determined by a few plain queftions, and
their anfwers. Firft, fince it is evident that the
hopes and comforts of Infidels are bound up in the
pleafures

pleafures and enjoyments of the prefent life; is it not undeniable, that any perfons, propagating a fyftem which tends to difturb their purfuits, interrupt their enjoyments, or leffen their confequence, muft render themfelves odious?

Is it in the power of the laws to fupprefs or controul the private hatred, or animofity, of Infidels againft their opponents?

Is it not alfo probable, that calumny and contempt will be made ufe of to ruin the credit of fuch perfons, who may innocently fuppofe the prefent life not to be the *ultimatum* of all their hopes and happinefs?

But while Chriftians might thus expofe themfelves to the perfecutions of Infidels, the probability that the latter would not be perfecuted in return; or that their retaliation would be confiderably lefs in proportion, than that of the former, is evident from various confiderations. For inftance;

The Chriftian, expecting a hearing before another tribunal, may bear with many offences and repeated wrongs; and, therefore, will be lefs liable than the Infidel to retaliate an injury upon his neighbour, or enemy.

He may alfo be quickened in this fpirit of forbearance, by the confideration, that he obeys one of the pofitive commands of the Gofpel; and that, by the patient endurance of other men's faults, he fhall the better enfure the forgivenefs of his own.

And, upon the fame belief, he may even go farther, by returning good for evil.

Now, as Infidelity acknowledges neither motives nor objects of this kind, its objections to Chriftianity, upon the ground of cruelty, or perfecution, are proved to have no real foundation in fact.

We

We have alfo been told, that the wifdom of a nation may be feen in its proverbs. To the advantage of Chriftianity, then, we may remark, that the Mahometans have an adage, expreffing that, " He who forgives an injury, does well ; but he " that revenges it, does better." A maxim this, which, however it may affimilate with Infidelity, militates againft both the letter, and the fpirit of the Chriftian religion.

Having done with the charge of perfecution, I muft advert to the Infidel's opinion of the *Reafon and fitnefs of things*, which they recommend as a ftandard to try the abfurdity of Chriftian doctrines ; and which, if we could give them credit, thefe gentlemen have the exclufive privilege of exhibiting to advantage. If fo, how is it that their demonftrations have been repeated, years after years, without effect ; and that people in general ftill reject their folutions of the phenomena around them? How is it that your notion of the origination of all things from a confufed mafs of atoms ;—that there is no other God than the univerfe ;—that all the men and animals, which deftroy each other, are only parts and modifications of the fupreme Being ;— that matter firft fet itfelf in motion ;—that man's fuperiority to the brute refults entirely from his organization ;—that he is like a piece of mechanifm, or a plant, and that when he dies, all dies with him :—I fay, what is the reafon that thefe opinions of yours, gain no more evidence than they have done, though they have wanted none of the advantages of rhetoric or elocution to recomend them to the world? How is it that thefe leaves, from your tree of knowledge, fo flattering to human vanity, meet with no more admirers? How is it that the great mafs of people do not join iffue with you in the

the fupport of thofe opinions, which are to free them from the fetters of their education, and the preffure of fuperftition and tyranny? But above all, How is it that your doctrines cannot deliver men from their perfonal vices and defects, and the predominance of evil habits and paffions? You muft acknowledge that, after all your perfeverance and indefatigable endeavours to enlighten them, they do not comprehend the magnitude and importance of your fchemes! otherwife, they could not reject them! What then becomes of your *Reafon and Fitnefs of things?* This queftion muft refolve itfelf into one of thefe folutions; " Either you " are *not fit* to teach;—or it is *not fit* that mankind " fhould be fo inftructed."

The fuperior efficacy of the Chriftian doctrine upon the minds, even of fuch men as are, or have been, immerfed in vice and folly, cannot be difputed, but by thofe who are enveloped in prejudices, which I have found as prevalent among Infidels as any defcription of Chriftians whatever.

One of the principal obftacles to your inftruction, I find to be, that flattering notion of Mr. Paine, " that every man's mind is his own church."

Some of you are ready to deify Mr. Paine for this difcovery;—but let me tell you, he was not the firft that broached this deleterious noftrum; it was in the mouths and writings of almoft all the fectarifts that diftracted this kingdom, between the reigns of Charles the Firft and Second. It is a principle, virtually acknowledged by the Quakers, and was very pointedly urged and infifted upon, by a perfon in the laft century, known by the appellation of Cobler How; in a pamphlet entitled, " The Sufficiency of the Spirit's Teaching;" and in plain fenfe, means very little more, than that
every

every man loves to be led by his own whims and fancies, as foon as ever he becomes a Diffenter from the eftablifhed order of the church. This explanation, I think, is well warranted by the conduct of thofe who have, from time to time, adopted the principle of *felf-fufficiency*.

In fact, fo far from anfwering the end propofed, either by Infidels or Sectarifts, I have generally obferved, that when this notion is reduced to practice, inftead of being fufficient for the teaching of all, it has been the principal reafon why none have been fufficiently taught! In cafes of common life, men naturally afk the advice of others, but here, in a concern of the laft importance, every man's knowledge is fuppofed fufficient for himfelf.

In no fingle point whatever has the ignorance of Atheifts and Deifts appeared fo glaring, as when they affect a capacity for Bible criticifm. Mr. Paine's obfervations, under this character, might be corrected by many fchool-boys. With him, neither metaphor nor allegory is allowable in religion! The Book of the Revelations he condemns at once as a book of enigmas; at the fame time, the 19th Pfalm, which is almoft a complete allegory, is, in his eftimation, a *Chef d'œvre!* In fact, if the ftyle of our religious inftructions could be fquared, according to the demonftrations of Euclid, at which Mr. Paine feems to hint, all his reproach upon the Quakers, about "a drab-coloured creation," as the refult of their tafte, would, with equal propriety, apply to himfelf. Several of Mr, Paine's notions are borrowed, but his criticifm is all his own.

The fmall number of Chriftians, in comparifon with the great majority of Pagans and Mahometans in the world, is an *objection*, I will not call it an *argument*, almoft idolized by Deifts and Atheifts.

ifts. It is, I acknowledge, formidable in its firft appearance; but, on a clofe infpection, it foon lofes its confequence. I will not only admit the relatively fmall number of Chriftians in the world, but that they are equally fmall among ourfelves, fo few there are who live up to the fpirit of Chriftianity. This conceffion, however, makes nothing againft the univerfality of the Chriftian Religion, but rather tends to its eftablifhment, becaufe, among Pagans and Mahometans, there are, on the other hand, many who, living above the dictates of thofe falfe fyftems, are, in the beft fenfe, true Chriftians. Hence, as it is expreffed in Acts x. v. 34, 35. " God is no refpecter of perfons, but " in every nation he who feareth him and work- " eth righteoufnefs is accepted with him."

Chriftianity, then, is more of a *principle* than a *profeffion*; yet any perfon who could undervalue the written word, upon this account, would juftly fall under the cenfure of the Apoftle, Romans, chap iii. v. 1, who infifts upon the advantage of the Jews over the Gentiles, " Chiefly, that " becaufe unto them were committed the *Ora-* " *cles of God.*" And unbelievers fhould notice, that the fame reafoning, ufed by the Apoftle, all through the fecond chapter of the Romans, is exactly applicable to thofe perfons who, at this time, enjoy the light of revelation, and others who poffefs it not. Vain then, are the efforts of Infidels, as they fay, to *fimplify Religion ;* and futile the attempt to magnify *Reafon,* by fuppofing the *Light of Nature,* and the *Revelation of the Gofpel,* to be one and the fame! Volney, for this purpofe, refers me to the remains of Egyptian antiquities; I examine them, and am difappointed. As well might the bigotted Papift appeal to the exterior and venerable appearance of fome Gothic ftructure; which

may

may be furveyed by the rational with a figh, while it is worfhipped by the fuperftitious: the former, penetrating its inmoft receffes, might fcrutinize the character and principles of the original accupants. The obfervations of the latter, would probably extend no farther than the monuments, the ramifications of the columns, the ftoried windows and the length of the aifles! And, as in many old manfions, fome apartments are kept locked up, under the pretext that they are haunted; fo, the pretended myfteries of ancient Paganifm, like the rooms in thefe old manfions, are found, upon the opening, to contain very little, befides antiquated duft, or ufelefs lumber.

And now, oh! ye Reformers of ancient opinions, if your leaders are thus fuperficial and ignorant, how is it with thofe that are led? The latter, for implicit faith, are not furpaffed by any of the Chriftians you condemn. Among thefe, as faith is defigned to eftablifh an object, it produces and preferves unanimity. Among you, as your negative belief is only calculated to remove every reftraint, except individual whim and caprice, difcontent and difcord ultimately follow. Where all wifh to command there is none to obey. Thus you neither " enter into reft yourfelves nor fuffer others; you can " neither feek peace nor enjoy it." Within your own pale, having no crimes or failings which you dare condemn, you are compelled to feek them in others! Where every one is a malefactor, none can affume the office of cenfor or judge. Where nobility of mind, is not admitted, all are confidered as bafe; and, having no fcope for acrimonious propenfities at home, this reftraint only tends to fharpen the daggers you prepare for others, and render them ftill more deftructive. No longer, of any confequence to each other, you can hope for no importance,

portance, but in proportion as you diftinguifh your felves by the inroads which you make upon religion, as your common enemy.

Like the Indian warriors who recommend themfelves by the number of fcalps they bring in, fo muft you exalt yourfelves, or fink into abfolute infignificance. Similar to the fallen fpirits, you have no longer any confolation but in manifefting your enmity againft all who have not involved themfelves in your revolt. Unwilling to *ferve* in the *Heaven* of Religion, you feem determined to *reign* in the *Hell* of your own licentioufnefs; and, having broken from your original orbit, the harmony and brightnefs of fuperior intelligences, no longer excite in you, the correfpondent fenfations of delight and concord.

This parallel, founded upon no fiction, but upon a fober truth, I fhall carry no farther, than to obferve, that while the fallen fpirits are admitted to be eminent for their *knowledge,* you, not deficient in pride, are the moft confpicuous for your *ignorance.*

Into fuch a community as theirs, who would wifh to enter, or who, made fenfible of its fpirit and tendency, would wifh to remain? What credit or fafety can be expected where, religion being excluded, all the bad paffions are let loofe, or but feebly confined by the flender tie of human convenience? Will thofe who look upon every action, as the refult of a felfifh or interefted motive, refpect either merit or virtue in others? Where virtue has no intereft, it has, of courfe, no influence. Where depravity is under no check, excellence is of no value. Where fuperiority creates no generous emulation it is the caufe of envy. And where benevolence fails to excite gratitude, it only ftings the receiver with a malignant, or uneafy fenfe of his inferiority, and the motives of the donor are conftrued into

fel-

felfifhnefs. Perhaps this is the reafon that, among
the difciples of the New Philofophy, *Public Chari-
ties* are looked upon a *Public Robberies*. The vifionary reformers of the prefent day have alfo an idea
that the ftate can pofitively prevent *perfonal* and *individual* wretchednefs!

The genuine philofopher will not be furprized
at the contention, and privation of real happinefs
among herds of men, equally pretending to philofophy! If petty fqabbles and antipathies, in the
literary world, have juftified the poet's obfervation
of the natural enmity of wits and authors, a number comparatively fmall, what is to be expefted
from a whole community of would-be wits and
rival philofophers? Till modern philofophy came
in with its *moral equality*, other civil bodies ufed
to be compofed of head, feet, hands, and other
fubordinate and correfpondent members; but here
is a community that wifhes to be *all head!!!* Under the contemplation of this chimerical idea, it
is difficult to name the fenfations which it excites.

Before Deifm and Scepticifm became fafhionable, or were rarified into Atheifm; and particularly, when the former was here and there, the
opinion of fome fpeculatift, or folitary enthufiaft;
ftanding in the fame relation to multiplied Infidelity
as natural, to artificial fociety; the fpirit of piety,
like the ruftic virtues and artlefs fimplicities of un-
polifhed life, would fomtimes accompany its wanderings. Unconnefted with the " corrupt majority" it might then breathe its guilelefs effufions,
to him whofe temple it conceived " all fpace,"
Still, under the mildeft defignation we can be-
ftow, this is a branch, indigenous only to the
waftes of fociety, and can never be grafted
upon the common ftock To defcend from
figure; the moft innocent of Infidel opinions, once
liberated from the brain that conceived them, and
left

left to operate, as they *recently have done*, upon large and mixed multitudes, can never be accounted for; the multitudes being ever difpofed to carry thefe theories to extremes never thought of by the theorift, in whofe clofet they originated. The circumftance of thefe domeftic opinions being acted upon, by a political revolution abroad, as I have before hinted in the introduction to this work, has alfo given them a feature, altogether unknown in the annals of this country.

It is a mere quackery, in religion or morals, to prefcribe reafon only, as a fpecific for the numberlefs difeafes of the human mind. Wax is hardened and diffolved by the fame fun. Nor are all men, as the Atheifts dream, equally difpofed to virtue and probity, or even capable of the fame intellectual attainments. If it were not deemed a crime, by Infidels, to quote Scripture authority, one might fend thefe modern fmatterers in philofophy to that excellent Parable of the Sower, in the New Teftament, in which they may find an infallible theory of the moral capacities or incapacities of the human kind. Though I fhould not have referred them to Parables, by any means, had I recollected their common prejudice againft thofe parts of the Gofpel, as being purpofely intended to *obfcure*, and not *illuftrate*, the truths they fhould convey! A mode of reafoning they would not dare apply to the Fables of Æfop; though as our Lord makes no ufe of the perfonification of trees, birds, beafts, &c. between the perfpicuity and fimplicity of the one and the other, there is no comparifon. The perverted tafte of Mr. Paine, for literal inftruction only, has led his imitators to think little of thofe fuperior, and more ftriking modes of impreffing doctrinal truths, exhibited in the Parable of the good Samaritan, and others contained in the New Teftament. Yet that

that thefe ferpentine difpofitions, which have no
zeft for fublime truths, fhould recoil from the
depofitories, in which they are preferved, is more
the fubject of regret, than aftonifhment!

Even the reading of prophane hiftory, through
the medium of your opinions, but too frequently
ftrengthens very hurtful prejudices. General
charges and infinuations againft religion, and religious men, are not unfrequent among Hiftorians,
efpecially the moderns. But before you proceed
upon fuch fhallow grounds, it is neceffary to
weigh the decifion of one of your own oracles,
Mr. David Hume. The practice of arguing
againft any profeffion, from the abufe of it, comes
from you with a very ill grace, after he has af-
ferted, that, " This fophifm is one of the groffeft,
" and, at the fame time, the moft common to
" which men are fubject." He alfo obferves,
that, " the hiftory of all ages offers examples of
" the abufe of religion ; but thofe who would
" thence draw an inference to the difadvantage
" of religion in general, would argue very rafhly
" and erroneoufly. The proper office of religion
" is to reform men's lives, to purify their hearts, to
" enforce all the moral duties, and to fecure obe-
" dience to the laws and civil magiftrate. While
" it purfues thefe falutary purpofes, its operations,
" though infinitely valuable, are filent and fecret,
" and feldom come under the cognizance of hif-
" tory. The hiftorian, therefore, has fcarcely any
" occafion to mention any other than that adul-
" terate fpecies of it, which inflames faction,
" animates fedition, diftinguifhes itfelf upon the
" open theatre of the world, &c. and he may
" retain the higheft regard for true piety, even
" while he expofes all the abufes of the falfe.
" He may even think he cannot better fhew his
" attachment to the former than by detecting the
" latter

" latter, and laying open its abfurdity and per-
" nicious tendency."

To proceed farther, with refpect to the mental in-
devotion of the new philofophers ; if the mind can
conceive a continual effervefcence, or figure to
itfelf a family of children in perpetual warfare
with their parents, it might have fome idea of
the temper and difpofition of modern Infidels
towards the Great Creator. While Chriftians
thank him for their creation, the former do not
think their prefervation worthy an acknowledge-
ment ! In fact, deeper in degeneracy, than any
of their predeceffors, through having more light,
they have made themfelves intire ftrangers to the
fpirit, or exercife of devotion towards any object
of fupreme worfhip. Averfe to praife, and only
alive in cenfuring the harmony and beauties of Creation, Mr. Edmund Burke's idea, of " the heart
" of a thorough-bred metaphyfician, the cold
" malignity of an evil fpirit, and not the frailty
" and paffion of a man," is by no means harfh,
when applied to you !—To the fond hopes and en-
dearing conceptions of the Chriftian, you naturally
oppofe the petrifying refiftance of the Torpedo !
Thus fallen, your mention of the names of a Socrates, or Antoninus, is a profanation. To pafs
over your degrading fentiments of the Divinity,
not the regions of Siberia and the gardens of
Hefperus can produce a ftronger contraft, than
the chilling influence of your opinions, fet in competition with any kind of worfhip, or internal
reverence, of which we can conceive !

" Go, then, contracted Infidel ! withdraw thy-
" felf ftill farther from the views and comforts of
" thy fellow-men. Still, confined within thy own
" narrow fphere of reflection, perfuade thyfelf thou
" art not made for immortality. Avail thyfelf,
" then, by any means, of all the advantages of
" the

" the prefent life: add to thy eftimation of every
" perifhable good; and, ftifling fympathy for the
" fufferings of others, let thy *own accommodation*
" fupercede every other confideration. Regard-
" lefs of the awards of pofterity, leave it to poets
" and orators, to dignify the defire of immortality,
" as the paffion of great minds: tell them, the
" philofopher, who calculates the refult of human
" actions, is not to be duped with pompous
" phrafes. Reply to them, that, thoufands have
" perifhed for their country, at Rome and Car-
" thage, whofe names are forgotten. Perfuade
" thyfelf, that vices, rather than virtues, tend to
" immortalize a name; and, that the records of
" hiftory prefer thofe who have defolated the
" earth. Tell the advocates for humanity, that
" the majority of Heroes have been Tyrants; and
" to others, leave the folly of fowing where they
" fhall never reap.

" From the darkeft corner of the intellectual
" world, thus continue, like the envenomed fpider,
" to envelope thyfelf, and all intelligent beings in
" the cobweb-chains of neceffity. Believe, if thou
" canft, that every action, as well as the means for
" obtaining its object, is impelled by a firft caufe:
" and that even the hand of a murderer is only a
" feeble link in the great concatenation of events!
" Go on,—but I will withdraw from this precipice,
" from whence we cannot look down, but with hor-
" ror and dizzinefs."

Having now fhewn the invalidity of the expectation of Infidels, that any change of the political
fyftem would be more favourable to their opinions
than the prefent; that, under the pretext of improving the faculty of Reafon, their neglect of proper
means to ftimulate and apply it, has a certain,
though indirect, tendency to deftroy the end propofed.

Having

Having refuted the charges of cruelty, and a perfecuting fpirit in the Chriftian Religion, and urged feveral arguments to prove its humanity, fuperior to the Mahometan or Infidel fyftem.

Having made it appear that the condition of Infidel Society, is neceffarily a ftate of warfare and competition, fubverfive of good order, difcouraging to merit, and deftitute of proper motives to excite emulation, or prevent a degeneracy of principle and practice : Having fhewn the danger and novelty of relation, in which thefe focieties were placed by political events, the *Quackery of Reafon* as an univerfal medicine in morals, and the groundlefs prejudices of unbelievers againft the parables of the New Teftament.

And laftly, having demonftrated their total want of devotional tafte, or veneration of the Supreme Being, or any form of worfhip, I fhall for the prefent, profecute thefe charges no farther.

If it be faid, that I have lighted up the beacons of alarm, it is granted ; but I have invoked no perfecution, nor imprecated any greater punifhment upon the opinions I explode, than the contempt, and the caution, this expofure muft neceffarily produce.

Detached from any *political agency*, the momentary triumphs of individual, or collective, infidelity, are neither to be envied nor feared. It is a painful pre-eminence, and Infidels well know it, when they again wifh that to be *true*, which they had perfuaded themfelves was *falfe !* Nor let the reader be furprifed, that I have claffed Atheifts and Deifts indifcriminately : for the common practice of Infidels, to cover themfelves with the name of *Deifts*, is a mere pretext, calculated to efcape the more odious appellation of *Atheifts*. For thofe who will not admit of God's moral government of the world ; nor allow mortals any knowledge of his attributes ;

or

or who deny, the immortality of the foul, I fay, whatever fuch perfons may think to the contrary, their notions can never prefent to the *minds* of the *impartial*, any other ideas than thofe of *doubt*, and a privation of every degree of worfhip or affection ; if they do not even exhibit an object of *abfolute averfion* or *contempt :* fo that between fuch Deifm as this, and ftark Atheifm, there may be a nominal *diftinction*, but no *difference*. This idea was very juftly appreciated by the Bifhop of London, in his Charge to the Clergy of his Diocefe, in 1794. Speaking of the French ; they were, faid he, " pre-" tended Deifts, but real Atheifts. And although " the name of a Supreme Being was fometimes " mentioned, yet it was feldom mentioned but with " ridicule and contempt. They acknowledged " nothing beyond the grave ; and they ftigmatifed " all opinions different from thefe, with the names " of fuperftition, bigotry, prieftcraft, fanaticifm, " and impofture.

Thefe dangerous opinions were rendered more illufive, by the great names that fanctioned them ; but as none of them are more familiar than that of Voltaire, I would caution the young and unwary, againft any feductive influence upon this head. It is wrong, in the Infidels, to oppofe, as they do, the *difbelief* of the French Wit, to the *belief of Chrift-ianity* by the immortal Newton. For, granting that Voltaire deferved the panegyric of a German No-bleman, who entitles him " the divine Magician " whofe breath diffipated the thick cloud that " covered all Europe, and obferves, that happier " in his attempts than Orpheus, he did not ftop at " humanizing the furies, but metamorphofed the " monfters of intolerance, fanaticifm, and blood, " into humane and fociable beings :" I fay, unlefs it could be proved that thefe monfters, againft whom this giant of French literature exerted

himfelf

himfelf, were the *legitimate offspring of Chriftianity*, thefe pompous phrafes mean nothing.
But till the tolerating fpirit of Proteftants, and
the perfecuting genius of the Church of Rome,
be proved one and the fame, the Chriftianity *believed* by Newton, and *difbelieved* by Voltaire, will
remain as effentially different as light and darknefs.

The Rev. Mr. Fellowes, in his Chriftian Philofophy, with others I could mention, are of the
opinion, that the late enmity of the French Infidels,
againft Chriftianity in *general*, was at firft excited
by the *particular* enormities and corruptions of the
Romifh Church, " which accumulating for cen-
" turies, at laft produced a monfter, which devoured
" its mother. The Deiftical philofophers might,
" fays he, have haftened its birth, but they had no
" fhare in its formation. Had they been the ef-
" fential caufe of the decline of Chriftianity, the
" fame caufe exifting ftill, would have prevented
" its revival ; but the beft informed travellers affure
" us, that Infidelity itfelf is declining, now the
" caufe, which produced it, is no more."

More, and undeniable evidence of this decline,
and the confequent revival of Chriftianity in France,
has fince been brought forward by the invitation
given by Bonaparte, to the return of the Clergy ;
the opening of a greater number of churches, and
his own attendance in perfon, at divine worfhip.
The conductors too of the public prints, who,
during Robefpierre's tyranny, had profeffed themfelves
Atheifts, though all of them may not be fincere in
their recantation, acknowledged their faith in
Chriftianity, in the courfe of March, 1800 ; a circumftance, fufficiently indicating the altered ftate of
the public mind in the French nation.

Now, as a collateral proof of the remarks by Mr.
Fellowes, which were written in 1798, it feems this
decline

decline had made such progress in the summer of
1799, as to occasion the shutting up of the Theophilanthropic Temple, and the opening of several
churches in the French capital. But without rest-
ing upon these events, as facts, there are several natural reasons, from which a true philosopher may
infer, " that the Christian Religion, stripped of its
" abuses, will take a deeper root than before, in
" the minds and affections of the French people.
" Nor is it unworthy of remark, that the late Rev. Mr.
" Fletcher, of Madeley, wrote a letter from Macon,
" in Burgundy, in 1778, in which he observed, that
" Popery would fall in France in this or the next
" century." He adds, " I make no doubt, God
" will use those vain men (the Voltaires, Rousseaus,
" Mirabeaus, &c.) to bring about a reformation
" here, as he used Henry VIII. to do that work
" in England: so the madness of his enemies
" will at last turn to his praise and the furtherance
" of his kingdom."

I shall only observe, that of the permanence of
this approaching change, no rational doubt can be
entertained. Having borne the last and most violent
shocks of Apostacy and Infidelity, no hope now
remains for the Infidel, that the light of Christianity
shall ever be extinguished, but with time itself. The
veil of pretended philosophy has been torn
asunder, and its features exposed to shame and de-
rision ; while the beauties of Religion have increased seven-fold. This bright constellation having
received its impetus from the hand of the Divinity,
no human effort can resist its progress. That it
may penetrate the darkest regions of the earth,
ought to be the sincere wish of every man, who
has the least pretence to sound reason or understanding.

POST-

POSTSCRIPT.

Chronological Sketch of the Origin, and Progreſs of Infidelity, in England, anterior to the French Revolution.—Remarks upon Profeſſor Robiſon.—New Illuſtrations of German Literature.—Beautiful Tranſlation from Profeſſor Ramler.—Vindication of the Sedition-Bills.—Declining State of Democratical Politics.—Phyſical and Moral Superiority of the Ariſtocracy in every Nation and Government.

As it is natural for the mind, when taking a view of any multiform, or mighty maſs of matter, to inquire from whence, or by what means, it accumulated, ſo, in reflecting upon the late increaſe of Infidelity in this country, I was led to conclude, that the developement of the various ſources of this evil could not be indifferent to a curious inveſtigator of men and manners.

However indiſputable the Rev. Henry Kett's aſſertion may be, "that the ideas of Infidelity, "which had been long floating in the world, were "firſt embodied into a practical ſyſtem of wicked- "neſs, by Voltaire, and others," I muſt ſtill beg leave to fix its æra in England, long before the writings of Bolingbroke made their appearance; this I muſt aſcribe to a period of hiſtory, which bears a nearer reſemblance than any other to recent tranſactions in France, *viz.* the period of the civil wars,

between

between Charles I. and his Parliament. Then churches were converted into stables, or ruins, and their minifters driven into exile; while their fucceffors were divided into various fects, alternately fupporting the moft abfurd, impious, and extravagant, opinions, whofe variety of creeds naturally tended to the difcredit of all religious authority.

During this period, I fay, it cannot be doubted, but as one extreme always produces another, fo the impiety and fanaticifm of the fixteenth century were as properly the parent of the Infidelity that fucceeded it, as the late maffacres and profcriptions in France were confequences of the rejection of the milder doctrines of the Gofpel; and the refult of a decree, that " death is an eternal " fleep!"

That much Infidelity did fucceed the civil wars of Charles I. was moft vifible in the licentious reign of his fucceffor; and may alfo be gathered from the many treatifes written againft avowed and unqualified Atheifm before the clofe of the fixteenth century: even the learned Dr. Henry More did not think the Atheifm of that time beneath his attention.

This monftrous feature, in the religious hiftory of this country, did not efcape the French writers; Boffuet in particular feems to treat Free-thinking, " as the laft refuge of minds tired out with reli- " gious wars, and the revolutions to which they " gave rife."

Charles II. Monfieur Grofley obferves, " either " through a fecret attachment to the Roman Ca- " tholic religion, or from views merely political, " favoured the Free-thinking turn of his fub- " jects."

James II. to increafe a toleration that fuited his purpofe, fuffered all the Latudinarians, among the
Noncon-

Nonconformifts, to efcape notice; and, in the reign of William III. it is obferved, that Shaftefbury and and his admirers thought very freely upon religious fubjects.

In 1696, John Toland publifhed his Chriftianity not Myfterious; a work publicly burnt in Dublin, as foon as it appeared; but, flying to England, the author and his book were left unmolefted.

Encouraged by this reception, in 1699, he publifhed the Life of Milton; in which, infinuating his doubts concerning the authenticity of the Old and New Teftaments, he next anfwered his numerous objectors, in another work, intituled, Amyntor.

The ineffectual oppofition made to thefe writings, by the inferior Clergy, affembled in convocation in 1702—*(See Life of Toland prefixed to his Works, in* 1725) only tended to increafe their popularity and reputation.

In 1705, the Works of Lord Herbert, of Cherbury, were firft publifhed in Englifh.

In 1713, Collins's Difcourfe upon the Rife and Growth of a Sect, called Free-thinkers, ferved to increafe the confequence of that party; the more fo, from the number of replies made to it by Dr. Bentley, and other Clergymen.

In 1716, it may be fuppofed, that Free-thinking had made fome progrefs in the genteel or literary world, as a very fenfible and well-written pamphlet made its appearance in behalf of the belief of a providence, &c. addreffed to the Wits, at Button's Coffee-houfe; not Addifon, Steel, or Arbuthnot, it is fuppofed, but fome of the minor geniufes.

In the reign of George I. Socinianifm, fo near a-kin to Deifm, was difclaimed by that monarch, who, as head of the church, publifhed a proclamation, prohibiting the diffemination of fuch writings

writings as were favourable to the new opinions concerning the Trinity.

The New Annual Register, for 1782, obferves, " that the firft and moft formidable attack upon " the Chriftian religion was made by Lord Her- " bert, of Cherbury. Collins, was afterwards fol- " lowed by Toland; and Tindal's Chriftianity, as Old " as the Creation, fucceeded to Morgan's Moral " Philofophy ; then came the more fubtle perform- " ance of Chriftianity not founded on Argument."

From Bifhop Gibfon's Paftoral Letter, in 1729, though principally directed againft Woolfton's Treatment of the Miracles, and the publications of Chubb, which immediately fucceeded, and con-tinued till 1749, it appears, that no refpite was fuffered to take place. It fhould alfo be ob-ferved, that, between 1730 and 1744, the firft period being that which produced the famous con-troverfy of the Refurrection, and the celebrated pamphlet, the Tryal of the Witneffes : there were three editions of a Deiftical Anfwer to the fame, by Mr. Peter Annet ; befides two other pamphlets written by him, *viz.* the Refurrection Reconfider-ed, and, laftly, the Refurrection Defenders ftripped of all Pretences. Thefe things, from the con-veniency of their price, and the zeal of the party who diftributed them, who, no doubt, confidered themfelves as a rifing Sect, certainly had their weight in fhaking the pillars of popular opinion, among the middling and lower ranks of men.

Under the reign of George II. " the philofophy " of Shaftefbury, became fo far predominant, that, " for a number of years, no book was more uni- " verfally admired, or more generally read, among " people of tafte and fafhion, than that nobleman's " Characteriftics."

Thefe

Thefe were fucceeded by the publication of Lord Bolingbroke's Effays, about the year 1754, by his friend Mallet; of whom Dr. Johnfon obferved, " that he difcharged the blunderbufs, the " noble author had left loaded, againft the religion " of his country." Queen Caroline, it is alfo reported, was favourably difpofed towards thefe heterodox opinions.

In Monfieur Grofley's New Obfervations, on England, in 1765, he obferves, that Catholics, Church of England men, Methodifts, &c. all make a common caufe againft a Sect which every day gains ground; I mean *Free-thinking*.

Relative to the original Debating Societies, perhaps the ultimate celebrity of the Robin Hood, the firft of thefe dangerous Schools of Eloquence, or the impatience of fome of its members to appear in print, was the caufe of the profecution of Peter Annet, one of its members, and his fentence of one year's imprifonment in Newgate, with an expofure in the pillory. Nor had the final difperfion of this Society, about 1773, fcarcely taken place, before the Infidel fyftem was transferred, with increafing attractions, into the clofet, by the fafhionable reception of the writings of Hume, and the daily improvements of Voltaire, D'Alembert, and the French philofophers in general.

The affociation at the Robin Hood, it cannot be doubted, had left the feeds of Infidelity deeply rooted in many of the members, who recollected the fpeeches of Annet; Dr. Lucas, of Dublin; and other orators of no mean talents. Among thefe people, the profecution of Annet was a frequent fource of converfation; while the kindnefs he experienced, from the amiable and ever memorable Archbifhop Secker, was forgotten, or only confined to the knowledge of a few.

During

During Annet's imprifonment, in Newgate, that worthy primate, I have been told, fent to make fome inquiry into his pecuniary affairs, and offered fome comfortable affiftance, which Annet, far advanced in years, did not live to enjoy; and from the following paffage of the prefent Bifhop of London's Review of the life of Archbifhop Secker, it appears, that Mr. Annet was not the only object of fuch generous treatment on the part of the primate. " Whenever any pub-
" lications came to his knowledge that were
" manifeftly calculated to corrupt good morals,
" or fubvert the foundations of Chriftianity,
" he did his utmoft to ftop the circulation
" of them: yet the wretched authors them-
" felves, he was fo far from wifhing to treat
" with any undue rigour, that he has more
" than once, extended his bounty to them in
" diftrefs." The tranflation of the whole works of Voltaire, and their repeated publication in fixpenny numbers, was alfo the means of put-ting the public in poffeffion of his plaufible dialogues between a Chriftian and an Honeft Man, a Caloyerian, &c. And thefe were again multiplied, when the complete fets being fold off, the remains were a fecond time diffeminated among an inferior order of readers, by their expofure upon the bookfellers ftalls, in common with fecond-hand magazines, at no more than one penny a number.

As under parts to the principal acts of Infi-delity, upon the grand ftage of literature, it might have been obferved, that, for near a cen-tury paft, Blount's Oracles of Reafon, Collins on the Free-thinkers, &c. have lain upon the bookfellers ftalls, courting the infpection of paf-fengers; and that, after the public had been
accommodated,

accommodated, in the fame way, with the wafte paper of Morgan, Mandeville, Annet, Chubb, and all the fecond race of Infidels, near half a century; by way of a more refined entertainment, the circulating libraries were fupplied with the Eloifa and Emilius of John James Rouffeau, and other tranflations from the French, equally fubverfive of good morals. To the literary abilities, above vulgar ken, we may add, thofe of Gibbon, the hiftorian; The Apology for the Life and Writings of David Hume, and that impertinent parade about his domeftic virtues, fo fmartly replied to by the late Dr. Horne; and, next to thefe, we might reckon the cheap editions of the Philofophical Dictionary, by Voltaire; printed at London and York.

Upon the whole, from the recollection of the remote concatenation here adduced, it may be prefumed, that Infidelity had attained a degree of *relative antiquity*, and thus impofed upon many, who would have rejected a *novelty*, as hazardous and queftionable.

But, after all, where Infidelity has failed of complete fuccefs, many upon whom it has operated have been, at leaft, brought under Socinianifm, the *Frozen Zone* of religion, even if it can deferve the name; for, before Dr. Prieftley had attained to his paft celebrity as a *divine*, this opinion undoubtedly had its effects in deadening the human heart. But, when his improvements upon it, were dignified with the name of *philofophy*, the warm tide of intellectual life immediately ceafed to flow. The character of a *materialift* was fixed, and all the benignant fources of genuine Chriftianity, which might have been expected in this quarter, were hermetically fealed.

It

It was this great chemift who reduced all the ideas of the grand enemy of the human race to a mere "*perfonification of human paffions;*" from whence, and fimilar refinements in what was called the "*corruptions of Chriftianity,*" a difcuffion of queftions, in the debating focieties, on a Sunday evening, previous to 1781, fubverfive of all the fundamentals of our religion, operated as a fufficient juftification of the Sunday Reformation-Bill, paffed in that year, which, by prohibiting the taking of money at the dcors, put a temporary ftop to the increafe of Infidelity in the lower orders.

But this hydra had too many heads to be crufhed at once; for, in 1786, it was remarked by Archdeacon Paley in his Moral Philofophy, " That Infi
" delity is now ferved up in every fhape that is
" likely to allure, furprize, or beguile, the imagi
" nation, in a fable, a tale, a novel, or a poem,
" in interfperfed or broken hints, remote and ob
" lique furmifes, in books of travels, of philofo
" phy, of natural hiftory, in a word, in any form
" rather than that of a profeffed and regular dif
" quifition."

As to focieties which fubfifted in the interval which I have gone over, that in Margaret-ftreet, Oxford-road, was the next, both in the order of time and in its publicity, to that of the Robin Hood. But neither the gentleman, then known by the appellation of the *Prieft of Nature*, and who delivered Deiftical lectures in his chapel, in 1775-6, nor his congregation, fhould, by any means, be ranked with thofe peftiferous clubbifts of late date ; although it unfortunarely happened that his renewal of a dangerous profeffion of falfe philofophy continued the concatenation of Infidelity nearer to the æra of the French Revolution, which,

which, afterwards co-operating with thofe principles, increafed the number of Englifh Infidels
beyond all precedent.

From the period when the above-mentioned
lectures, in Margaret-ftreet, had clofed, till the
publication of the Age of Reafon ; Deifm, and the
heterodox opinions of the times, feemed to have
taken up their laft refuge in a pretty numerous
circle, near Hoxton, among a kind of *Infidel Myftics*, known to ftangers, from the circumftance of
broaching their fentiments in fome writings and
public places, by the appellation of *Ancient Deifts*,
as well as from the profeffion of their belief in the
eternity of the univerfe, &c. This place, being
attended by fome perfons above the common line
of life, finally operated as a kind of vortex, which
naturally attracted the reftlefs and diffatisfied of
every fect within its circle. Here human learning
was declaimed againft, as one of the greateft enemies to human happinefs or the improvement of
the intellect, and dreams, vifions, and immediate
revelations, were recommended as a fubftitute!
The faculty of foretelling future events was alfo
infifted upon ; the difcernment of fpirits, by the
phyfiognomy, the voice, the gait, &c. together
with the poffibility of converfing with departed
fouls. In fact, thofe pretences were carrried fo far,
that any vifitor, not in the habit of hearing fuper-
natural voices, or not informed of the common
occurrences of the day, by the miniftration of
Angels, would have been treated as a novice and
a difciple of the loweft form.

It was by no means unnatural, that this af-
femblage fhould be made up of Alchymifts, Aftro-
logers, Calculators, Myftics, Magnetizers, Prophets, and Projectors, of every clafs. In fact,
this community feemed " to embrace all the ec-
                                    " centric

" centric modes, sectaries, visionaries, fanatics,
" enthusiasts, rationalists, and every other name,
" into which affectation, whim, folly, or caprice,
" divide the populace.

Several of the members of this society have dif-
tinguished themselves, in their habits and manners,
truly eccentric; but, as a description of them
would be too long for the present purpose, I shall
only observe, that, there was so little of real religion
in their composition, that it almost immediately
yielded to the stronger impulse of the French
Revolution, and terminated in the general conversion of the members into *politicians* and *in-
quirers after news.*

What has occurred among succeeding associations, since the period last mentioned, has been
sufficiently noticed in the former part of this
work.

Relative to Professor Robison's History of a
Conspiracy, &c. I shall now observe, that, after
the minute details, given by him and the Abbé
Barruel, of the object of the French and German affiliations, no persons, unless they are totally
absorbed in prejudice, can any longer affect to
look upon the relations of these authors, as
being raked together, merely to serve a party-
purpose.

Without the evidence which they have adduced,
it certainly would demand some stretch of credulity,
to admit that Deists and Atheists have associated,
near half a century, for the sole purpose, as Voltaire
expresses it, to " *Ecrazer l'Infame,*" *viz.* Crush the
Wretch, Christ! However, the only difference between the English and French Infidels, is, in the
term of their existence; the latter had arrived at
maturity, while the former, being anticipated in
their view, a salutary check was opposed to their
progress,

progrefs, before they were capable of feeling their
ftrength.

Every good member of fociety, now enjoying
the benefit of a ftate of internal tranquillity, or com-
paring it with the ftorms and convulfions of a neighbouring kingdom, will, next to Providence, blefs the
means of his prefervation ; ana, penetrated by the
advantages he enjoys, they will at leaft infpire him
with a tacit juftification of meafures, at firft, perhaps,
deemed harfh. I mean, thofe meafures which have
been adopted by a vigilant government, and which
have, undeniably, prevented the diforder and con-
fufion which muft have otherwife enfued.

The blind tools of a party, and fhallow politicians, may continue declaiming againft what
they deem unneceffary violations of the forms of
the conftitution, as if the executive could at all
time be ufeful without a difcretionary and a dif-
penfing power.

It is to very little purpofe, that fome people
argue, that, the modern democratic party has
really or apparently received the fanction of fome
refpectable names in this country, both in and out
of the fenate. But if any fuch perfons have
flattered themfelves, that a Parliamentary Reform
was the *real object*, and not merely the *ftalking-
horfe* of the focieties, their want of information
is really to be pitied. They muft have known
very little of the hatred borne to all the privileges
of birth or acquirements, or of the frenzy, which
fometimes raged in the brains of their humble
friends in the city, and eaftern fuburbs ; or how
impatient they were of the tardy proceedings in
St. Stephen's Chapel ; the fafety and continuance
of which was principally owing to an augmenta-
tion of the affociated Volunteer-Corps. Of courfe
they muft be ignorant of the obligations they are
under

under to thofe who directed this military force, and actually prevented the madnefs of democracy from a phaeton-like affumption of the reins of government; from whence the whole ifland might have been kindled into a combuftion more deftructive than the infurrection of Jack Cade, or any of the diforders of his fucceffors. I will even hazard the fuppofition, no Volunteer-Affociations being formed, that republican frenzy had proceeded fo far as to corrupt the Guards, and *feize* or *maffacre* the whole Houfe of Commons; or as many of them as they found fitting; could thefe madmen fuppofe any men, or fet of men, would have accepted of the government at their hands, reeking with the blood of the Senate? I truft there are none, who bear the name of Britons, fo loft to the dignity of the national character, or of a caft fo fanguinary or degraded. Of courfe, hating both the treafon and the traitors, the fhocking deed would have reverted, with tenfold vengeance and remorfe, upon the heads of the perpetrators; while its refults muft have juftified the moft afflicting, and, perhaps, unheard-of recrimination. I intimated, that the fafety of the fittings of the Houfe of Commons was owing to the formation of the Volunteer-Corps, while democracy raged in this metropolis. I repeat it: for, notwithftanding not more than one perfon, as far as I recollect, has been convicted of feducing the foldiery from their allegiance, fuch attempts, among the Clubbifts, were not cafual, but part of a fyftem conftantly acted upon. To mingle with, and to treat, the foldiery was as much a part of the duty, while the Clubs exifted, as it was to meet at the divifion-rooms; and reports of progrefs, in this undertaking, were conftantly made and applauded.

I may

I may neither have the abilities to pronounce, nor the consequence to substantiate, a panegyric upon eminent characters; but as the effects of measures are the best comment upon the abilities of the men who produced them, let us farther suppose, for argument sake, that, after the recent adoption of French revolutionary principles in this country, the government had delayed the punishment or prevention of any overt-act, till matters had proceeded as far as they were carried in 1780! Will any of their accusers, then, take upon them to say where the consequences would have ended? I will now hazard a contrast: the popular tumult of 1780, without any national views, and without any leaders to direct its movements, eventually cost the lives of two hundred persons; while the more recent desperate scheme, to overturn all the constituted authorities of this kingdom, has been baffled, by the mere imprisonment of less than half that number, many of whom were afterwards liberated.

That government in dispersing these societies, and hindering their re-organization, have acted upon the principle, that " prevention is better than punishment," I believe might be justified by some who have smarted most severely for their attachment to republicanism. The *diet*, and not the *imprisonment*, in the House in Cold-Bath-Fields, being their principal complaint. But even this was not permanent; it being now some months since the few confined for seditious practices have been put upon the allowance of state-prisoners, while their wives and families, in order that the innocent might not share the punishment of the guilty, have had an allowance from government of half-a-guinea, and fifteen shillings, per week.

But

But it is not impoſſible to add to the teſtimonies brought by Profeſſor Robiſon, as to the real views of the ſelf-named philoſophers: the following paſſage in the late Lord Orford's Letters, written in 1765, and which could not be brought forward to promote the views of a party, may now ſerve our purpoſe with double effect:

" The Dauphin, ſays he, will probably hold
" out very few days. His death, that is, the
" near proſpect of it, fills the philoſophers with
" the greateſt joy, as it was feared he would en-
" deavour the reſtoration of the Jeſuits. You will
" think the ſentiments of *the philoſophers* very odd
" ſtate-news; but, do you know who the philoſo-
" phers are, or what the term means here? in the
" firſt place, it comprehends almoſt every body;
" and, in the next, men, who, avowing war againſt
" Popery, *aim, many of them, at a ſubverſion of*
" *all religion; and ſtill many more at the deſtruc-*
" *tion of regal power*. How do you know this?
" you will ſay; you, who have been but ſix weeks in
" France, three of which you have been confined
" to your chamber. True: but in the firſt period
" I went every where, and heard nothing elſe;
" in the latter, I have been extremely viſited, and
" have had long and explicit converſations with
" many who think as I tell you, and with a few
" of the other ſide who are no leſs perſuaded that
" there are ſuch intentions. In particular, I had
" two officers here the other night, neither of them
" very young, whom I had difficulty to keep from
" a ſerious quarrel, and who, in the heat of the
" diſpute, informed me of much more than I could
" have learned with great pains." Vol. V. p. 123.

In addition to the more recondite collection of facts, which the Profeſſor has ſelected from the German language, I ſhall next notice a Memorial,
written

in 1733, upon Secret Affemblies: Vide, Des Hern Baron Von Holberg's ubrige Kleine Schriften, Copenhagen printed, 1755. In this work, fays Baron Holberg, " I deemed it neceffary to pub-
" lifh my Philofophical Confiderations upon the
" fubject of Secret Societies, becaufe it is no-
" torious, that, at this period, feveral of them exift
" in various parts of Germany, the propagation
" of whofe extravagant opinions feem calculated
" to excite defpair rather than devotion."

But whatever might have been the precife object of thefe Secret Affemblies, the ftriking fimilarity, which the Baron traces out between the caufes that led to the death of Charles I. of England, and thofe we have witneffed preceding the late French Revolution; I fay, whatever the views of the former might have been, he makes it appear, that, the proceedings of the Englifh regicides in that reign, like the recent commotions in France, caufed fome alarm, and the adoption of meafures of precaution in fome of the neighbouring ftates. We fee, fays Baron Holberg, (in his Confiderations before-mentioned) from an Ordinance, publifhed, Wintermonat, December 24, 1655, that our gracious Sovereign, Frederic III. ftifled the Secret Affemblies, of that period, in their birth; not fo much on account of the falfe doctrines which they taught, but for fear of the bad confequences ufually refulting from fuch private meetings; the effects of which, we had learned by experience. And farther, that what was, *at firft, only the bufinefs of the Clergy, or the Police, at length required the affiftance of the Military.*— The grand Rebellion of England, the Baron goes on to fay, has fupplied us with proofs of the effects of thefe divifions. That tragedy, which has occafioned fo much prejudice to Religion and
the

the State, had the fame kind of beginning, *viz.*
*Secret Affemblies, Attacks upon Public Worſhip,
Prophecies, The expectation of the Millenium, An
equal diviſion of Property, or the poſſeſſion of all
things in common. Cleicheit unter Menſchen zu
ſteſten, viz. the Inſtitution of Equality among
Mankind and the like!!!* His Daniſh Majefty,
therefore, thinking it neceffary to ufe a timely
preventative of the evil of Secret Societies, iffued
the following Ordinance againſt them:

" Wir Friedrick der Dritte, &c. thun hiemit
" kund und zu wiffen: Da unfere Vorfahren fo-
" wohl, als wir, es beſtandig unfere vornehmſte
" Sorge haben feyn laffen, dafs das heilige und
" wahre Wort Gottes rein und lauter erhalten
" und bewahret werde, fo haben wir doch er-
" fahren, wie der Meifter der den Weizen mit
" dem Unkraut zu unterdrucken und zu werder-
" ben fuchet, das heilige Predigtampt und Mi-
" niſterium in Verachtung zu bringen fuchet, in-
" fonderheit dadurch, dafs er durch heimliche und
" fchadliche Zufammenkunfte, die fo es nicht bef-
" fer verftehen, von unferer Kirche, und dem
" gebrauchlichen Gottefdienſt abzuleiten ver-
" fuchet. Daher is unfer ernſtlicher Wille und
" Befehl, an alle hohe und niedrige Obrigkeit,
" dafs fi darauf Acht haben, fo, wie fie es vor
" uns zu verantworten gedenken, &c."

To the following effect:

" We, Frederick III. &c. hereby declare, and
" make known: fince it has been the conftant care
" of our predeceffors, as well as ourfelves, to re-
" tain and preferve the true and facred Word of
" God in its purity; and as we have learned,
" that certain perfons are endeavouring to cor-
" rupt and to tread down the wheat with the tares,
" and to bring the Miniſtry and the facred offices
of

" of religion into contempt, efpecially by the means
" of fecret and fcandalous meetings, by which
" they endeavour to lead the ignorant and un-
" wary from the eftablifhed worfhip and practice
" of our churches: it is, therefore, our abfolute
" Will and Command, that all our Magiftrates pay
" the ftrifteft attention to thefe Secret Affemblies,
" as they will otherwife be refponfible to us for
" their neglect, &c."

That no doubt might remain, whether any of
the Secret Societies, hinted at by the Baron, were
political, it is fufficient to indicate, that, within a
very few years after, he thought them a proper
fubject for Satire in his Comedy, intituled, *Der
Politiche Kangieffer*, or, *the Political Pewterer ;* of
which, from Gottfched's German Theatre, I attempted an Englifh tranflation, for private amufement, fome time fince. Gottfched, it fhould be
obferved, caufed it to be tranflated from the
Danifh, between 1746 and 1750, under the title
above-mentioned; but, from fome fimilarity of the
piece, with our Upholfterer, I chofe to give it the
title of THE DEMOCRAT CURED, or, *the Upholfterer
of Dantzick.* The Baron defcribes the Club, of
which the Hero is a leading member, with fingular
humour and propriety, efpecially when contrafted
with the views and capacities of fome, who have
borne the name of Reforming-Societies, in this
metropolis. He alfo plies him with fuch a fuccef-
fion of embarraffments, in confequence of his being
impofed upon, with the belief that he is chofen a
Burgomafter, that he is only faved from deftroying
himfelf by an explanation made to him by a Mr.
Worthy, to whom, till then, he had refufed to
give his confent to marry his daughter, in confequence of his being *no politician!* In the *dé-
noüement* of the piece, the author makes him
order

order the burning of all his political pamphlets :
and he leaves the ftage, after moft appofitely obferving, " It is true, one may eafily condemn a
" government in theory, without having any idea
" of the practical part. So, to have a general
" notion of a Sea-chart, and to underftand the art
" of navigation, are two things effentially different.
" In reading political tracts, it is alfo eafy to ob-
" tain a facility in fpeaking upon a variety of
" fubjects ; but much more than this, is neceffary
" to underftand the conftitution of a country.
" From what has befallen me to-day, every per-
" fon, of the fame rank in fociety, may derive
" an exemplary conviction, that a man, who has
" no other capacity than that of cenfuring his
" fuperiors and governors, muft be totally unfit
" to adminifter in their places. For an illiterate
" Mechanic, to take upon him the office of a
" Statefman, is juft the fame as if the latter
" fhould affume the profeffion of the former with-
" out any previous inftruction."

Thus far, as to the fimilarity of caufes and
effects, and the general opinion of the friends
of good government, relative to Secret Societies,
in England, France, and Germany. As to the
variety of the means, adopted in thofe countries,
for promoting their purpofes, and the *few* made
ufe of by the Englifh Societies, the latter was
probably for want of time ; efpecially, if the
opinion, " That the Englifh generally improve
" upon the difcoveries made by the French," can
apply in this particular.

Profeffor Robifon has moft copioufly difplayed
the addrefs of the French and German Illuminati,
in qualifying their revolutionary poifon to all ftates
and conditions of men ; and has intimated, more
than once, that it was a principal object with
them,

them, to render the prefent ftate of fociety, odious,
by a fictitious difplay of the indolent pleafures of
the patriarchal life. It was their defign, as he ex-
preffes it, in page 161, of his Proofs of a Confpiracy, to make the head of every family, what
Abraham was, their Patriarch, Prieft, and unlettered
Lord ; and Reafon, the Code of Laws to all mankind. And, as an additional inftance of this difpofition, and the nefarious profanation of talents
made ufe of to promote it, my readers may take
the following tranflation from the French, felected
from an Imitation of the Pfalms of David, in
poetic profe, and like them in the Englifh, and
fome other Rubrics, infiduoufly adapted to each
day of the month :

" God of my Fathers ! when fhall the patriarchal
" ages revifit the earth ?

" Then were men worthy of thy prefence,
" and thou didft deign to vifit them with thy
" bounty.

" Then the ruftic altars, upon the facred moun-
" tains, were neither loaded with gold, nor ftained
" with blood.

" Then thy minifters, clothed in linen and
" crowned with flowers, were not eloquent;
" but their hearts were as pure and as fimple as
" their offerings.

" Then the father of the family, king of his
" houfehold, had no other fceptre but his paf-
" toral ftaff.

" Without fword or balance, he adminiftered
" juftice at the foot of an Oak, or before the
" door of his Cottage.

" Plain fenfe and an upright mind were his
" code of laws.

" Then Sincerity watched at the doors, and
" Security was an attendant at the bed.

" The

" The founds of the locks and keys of Suf-
" picion were not heard, in the evening or the
" morning.

" Then, Oh! my God, man added nothing
" to thy gifts, but received them as they came
" from thy hand:

" Blood never ftained his lips, neither was he
" preferved by the deftruction of ufeful and peace-
" able animals.

" Then was the marriage-union, formed in the
" face of Heaven, without a witnefs, and with-
" out a prieft.

" Then, in the perfon of his father, the fon faw
" his God, clothed in the human form.

" Then, Oh! God of my fathers, thy thunder
" flept at thy feet, and thy right hand was in-
" ceffantly held forth to blefs thy children.

" Then thou didft not repent of thy work;
" but the minds of men were like a fpotlefs
" mirror, in which thou waft pleafed to multiply
" thine image.

" It is time, Oh! Lord, that thou fhouldft re-
" ftore thofe days upon the earth; that ferene and
" beautiful period, which fhould be had in ever-
" lafting rememberance."

Upon the abufe of French and German literature, I fhall dwell no longer. To this there are
many brilliant exceptions, particularly, a pamphlet,
publifhed in 1794, entitled, *Blick auf die Fran-
zofiche Revolution—Von einem Freunde des Volkes
und der Regierungen."* As far as this untranflated
" View of the French Revolution, by a friend to
mankind and governments," exhibits the origin of
that inexhauftable event, in caufes, never likely
to occur in England, I fhall quote a few paffages,
after premifing, as the moft oftenfible part of my
apology for fo doing, that no farther knowledge

of

of the author may be neceffary, than what is to
be collected from the following note at the bottom
of page 112. Alluding to the French Emigrants,
it is there faid:

" Since there are nobles of the prefent day who
" perfuade themfelves, that none but perfons of
" equal rank have a right to decide upon points of
" honour, we wifh to remind them, that our author
" is no lefs known by his fword than his pen ; that
" he is no ftranger in the Cabinet or the field ; and
" that, in refpect to birth, he might challenge the
" moft ancient and illuftrious houfes."

" It would, fays this noble author, be a glorious
" example to the world, fhould a great nation
" awaken inftantaneoufly, after many ages of fervi-
" tude and indifference, and, with true magnanimity,
" trace fociety up to its original fource, found its
" rights upon the principles of eternal juftice, and,
" at the fame time, poffefs fufficient wifdom to keep
" them under the dominion of reafon, confining
" even liberty itfelf within inviolable limits.

" But who is capable of cementing an union
" between extremes fo diftant from each other, as
" inflexible prudence and violent enthufiafm ? It
" is highly probable, that a nation, giving itfelf
" up to the guidance of philofophers, would be
" wanting in that energy, which alone is capable
" of overturning the thrones of defpotifm and pre-
" judice. This energy, is the fole inheritance of
" the paffions. On the contrary, if this nation
" fhould confift of men, animated with the fpirit
" of liberty, men, who had encountered and fuper-
" feded every difficulty, can it be fuppofed, that,
" while flufhed with fuccefs, they will liften and
" implicitly adhere to the difpaffionate voice of
" that reafon, which places true liberty under the
" dominion of the laws, and fixes the welfare of
                                    " civilized

" civilized fociety, in almoft an intire facrifice of
" the natural independence of man?

" The fame genius which plans a revolution
" fhould conduct its progrefs; the fame hand
" that breaks the fetters of a nation fhould be
" fufficiently powerful to reftrain its paffions; but
" the revolutions of ftates, however fagacioufly
" planned, are fubject to fo many accidents, and
" attended with fo much ambition, and private
" intereft, that they frequently take a bias, in di-
" rect oppofition to the views of the firft mover.
" This was eminently the cafe with the French
" Revolution, the origin of which, we muft feek
" not in its vifible epoch, but look back to times
" far remote."

I fhall wave this author's unqualified invectives
againft the French Emigrant Nobleffe, as the
caufe of moft of the calamities of their country;
to introduce his energetic defcription of the fall of
Robefpierre.

" At the moment this pamphlet is going to prefs,
" Robefpierre, is overthrown by a clap of thunder;
" his guilty blood flows upon the fpot where that
" of the benevolent Louis, Marie Antoinette, and
" feveral others, was fhed. Divine juftice feems
" to have referved him for this fpecial retaliation;
" this alone purfued him, and men were merely
" paffive in the execution of its fentence. Hu-
" manly fpeaking, the condemnation of Robef-
" pierre was by no means legal; even his murder-
" ers were partakers in his guilt, though they
" accufed him of original, unatonable, and even
" improbable crimes. In fact, his death feemed
" to have been demanded by the howling of the
" Furies, and merely a confequence of the appli-
" cation of his own principles, and that denial of
" refponfibility, which led to the execution of the

8   " King.

" King. It was the Firſt of September, turned
" againſt himſelf; thoſe cannibal taƈtics which
" muſt ſtill be repeated, to clear the earth of thoſe
" monſters, to whom they have been familiar."

This author, a ſtrenuous advocate for the conſtitution of 1791, as a proof of the futility of all
democratic revolutions, is forced, unintentionally,
to pay a compliment to the Britiſh Conſtitution,
through his panegyrics upon that which approximates towards it, the neareſt of any : and he, at
the ſame time, demonſtrates the vanity of every
attempt to deviate from that line, to which, even
the French nation, is neceſſarily returning. If the
politics of 1791, ſays he, ſhould ever obtain a
predominance, after a thouſand faƈtions have had
their day, they will infallibly convince the French,
that their true happineſs, is equally as diſtant from
a licentious liberty, as from an authority without
bounds or limits.

While ſome writers ſeem inclined to carry their
prejudices againſt German literature too far, it is
but juſt to obſerve, that the reign of the late Emperor Joſeph ſeemed to inſpire ſome of the authors
of that period with true Engliſh notions of government. Far from the degrading ſentiments of the
Illuminati, their opinions add a dignity to human
nature ; and, as genuine liberty is never ſpoken of
in any part of the known world without ſome reference to *England,* or *Engliſhmen,* ſome obſerva-
tions from a ſmall German traƈt, publiſhed at
Vienna in 1781, intituled, The Creed of a Citizen
of the Nineteenth Century, as they may pleaſe, as
well as flatter, our vanity, cannot be diſagreeable.

" I believe, ſays the anonymous author, that
" the maxim, that we are under no obligation to
" a bad government, and that one may violently
" deprive

" deprive a tyrant of life, is fcandalous, falfe, and
" blafphemous.

" I believe that the laws cannot be better ex-
" preffed than through the will of an upright and
" virtuous Regent.

" I believe that unlimited liberty is a chimera."

" I believe, that if Rome had not deftroyed Car-
" thage, Carthage would have deftroyed Rome. See
" an illuftration of this in England and her ene-
" mies. If England does not lofe her *fuperiority*
" *at fea*, it is evident, that with refpect to com-
" merce, *all other powers muft become her vaffals*.

" I believe the courage of an Englifhman never
" forfakes him. Expofed to the utmoft danger, he
" will improve the fituation. If the country muft
" be ruined, he will fay, rather to-day than to-
" morrow.

" I believe the abilities of any perfon in Geome-
" try, may be equalled by another ; the folution
" of problems being founded in certain data. But
" that in politics, there are no felf evident proofs,
" which neceffarily lead to other truths : all depends
" upon genius.

" I believe there are cafes when it is neceffary
" for a Prince to fet himfelf above the laws ; to alter,
" and even infringe them. But if he is prudent,
" he will neither tear, nor obliterate the picture,
" but only give it a new face."

It is to be lamented that feveral authors in Germany, enjoying the character of fine writers, have,
with Wieland, enlifted under the banners of Infidelity. Religion, however, is not left without a
witnefs in the genius of that country. The reader
of tafte will excufe my attempt in tranflating the
following beautiful fpecimen of the true fublime,
from a German verfion of Pfalm xix. by Profeffor
Ramler.

The

THE heav'nly concave's everlafting frame,
The azure canopy where meteors flame,
The felf-pois'd earth beneath, and thefe accord
To join in owning their eternal Lord.

Day fpeaks his praife, in heaven's all-chearing light,
Repeated by a thoufand tongues at night;
All nations learn the mighty theme to fing;
All look with rapture to the day's bright King.

His prefence, fhining thro' th' etherial round,
Draws the dark foreft from the earth profound;
The dew-fraught clouds, he from th' ocean fills,
Diftill'd anew, or ftream'd adown the hills.

A verdant robe, he for the earth prepares,
Bedeck'd with flower's, whofe various tiffue bears
Each hue, that on his cloud-wrought cincture glows,
The azure violet, or crimfon rofe.

His purple Throne he in the Eaft difplays;
His vaft domain unwearied he furveys;
Unnumber'd realms are in his circuit blefs'd,
His courfe triumphant, ends in glorious reft.

From his exhauftlefs fea of lambent light,
He richly fills the filver orb of night;
The morning ftar, and brother choir advance,
And, wreath'd with rays, perform their myftic dance.

Thro' boundlefs fpace, thus Sun and Stars proclaim
Th' Almighty hand, that form'd this wond'rous frame;
And, for his praife their rapid wheels employ'd,
For ever rolling thro' the mighty void.

I fhall now leave the merits and defects of our continental neighbours, to fhew by what means we have avoided the rocks, upon which others have fplit. With refpect to the Democratical Faction, much indeed is owing to the vigilance of Minifters in faving the country from

" *Oratores novi, ftulti, adolefcentuli.*"

Still, other caufes co-operating, feem to have fixed the fafety of this country, from the attacks of its domeftic enemies, upon an immoveable bafis; and
have

have thus contributed to the gradual, but certain extinction of that hot spirit, which has caused so much alarm to the lovers of good order and that subordination, by which, it can only be supported.

In the first place, every degree of confidence which the London Corresponding Society reposed in the nobility and others, who, for a time, gave into the idea of universal suffrage, and annual, or triennial, parliaments, has been rapidly declining ever since their Association refused to come into the measures of the Whig Club; the proposal of which, by the latter, engendered that dislike which afterwards increased in proportion as the Reforming Societies imbibed the doctrines of *civil* and *moral* equality.

Secondly, divisions and mutual distrust among members, occasioned by the punishment of some of the number, the dread of the same fate, and the great loss of time requisite for serving the various offices. But another circumstance which contributed to hasten the crisis of the dissolution of this body, was, the introduction of the *United Men* into the metropolis, in 1797 and 1798 ; or rather the toleration of such persons in the London Corresponding Society, as joint members of both ! I say the toleration, because the known violence of the former, caused them to be eyed with so much suspicion, that one division of the London Corresponding Society, was denied admission at the house of a member, only for writing a letter to one of the *United Societies.*

The grand arcana of this new establishment was always acknowledged to the *initiated*, " as to form " a diversion in favour of the enemy, in case of a " landing." Many persons also undertook to learn the French language, no doubt, with a view of facilitating a communication.

That

That the *United Men* should be obnoxious to numbers of the London Corresponding Society may not be easily credited by strangers; the fact, however, which I have stated, must be admitted; for, if both of these associations were hideous or unnatural, still, a dissimilarity, might exist between them; such as is hinted in a German History of Apparitions, one of whom is described as being so exceedingly terrific, as to affright other spectres!

Notwithstanding, as the procuring and learning the use of arms were the ground work of the association of the *United Men*, numbers of the London Corresponding Society, who did not relish these daring measures, very prudently withdrew from both associations. The government's knowledge of these several circumstances, is, in my opinion, a sufficient vindication of the necessity of the Bills against Sedition, and the Suspension of the Habeas Corpus Act.

But farther, no accurate observer can possibly be ignorant, how much the herding principle has been checked by an unprecedented price of provisions; I speak only of the lower classes : the beer-houses which, previous to the late rise of the necessaries of life, used, in working neighbourhoods, to be filled three evenings out of the six, have been gradually deserted. The passengers, who, in the piping times of peace, were frequently obstructed, can now pass, unmolested by ballad singers, and drunken squabbles in the streets, while the number of night charges at the watch-houses have decreased in proportion : and this accidental alteration of circumstances, by compelling mechanics and others to share their porter at home with their families, has prevented many of them from being introduced to the Infidel or Political Societies, at the public houses. As for the seceding and repentant clubbists;

bifts, many of them are not a little aftonifhed at their credulity, in being led away by men, only intent upon the difplay of their oratory, or filling their pockets at the expence of the public opinion. Nor will it foon be forgotten, that fome perfons of opulence, who had been clamorous for democratic diftinction, were afterwards implicated in charges of monopoly and oppreffion ; and, that during the late exceffive dearth of provifions, the principal part of the public charity did not flow from men, before in the habit of haranguing the populace upon their *real grievances*, but from others, generally in *oppofition* to fuch principles and proceedings ! Another final mean of damping the revolutionary fpirit, in the Societies I have been fpeaking of, was the recollection, that in their corporate economy, viz. in the petty adminiftration of their affairs, though there were no millions unaccounted for, yet there were many and repeated defaulters, and dilapidations of a leffer amount, clearly demonftrating that *Citizens* and *Minifters* in *miniature*, forming the *Executive Committee*, or acting as Secretaries, have been the firft to fecure *their own interefts*. And farther, when called to account for this *un-citizen like* behaviour, have even denied the right of refponfibility, and withheld or deftroyed the documents which might have been brought againft them !

But, notwithftanding thefe leffons, a delirium feems to have attached to, and never to have left the divided remains of Englifh Democracy, till it received the fhock of Bonaparte's conftitution ! Otherwife, the voice of Reafon, added to the former changes in the French government, muft have been heard ; or even thofe revolutions would have filently deftroyed all the ideal and imitative frames, which the Conftitution-builders had been laying

for

for years on this fide of the water, and have forced
them back upon their own, though by a negative
preference.

But in fpite of the difcouraging fpecimens exhibited to the London Correfponding Society and their
adherents, *viz.* by their *Executive Committee*, and
other mimic minifters ; while they flattered themfelves that the foundations of Republicanifm ftood
fure in France, a cure was always expe&ed in the
old revolutionary mode of *changing men.* It was
to little purpofe that the focieties were deterred
from meeting : that their difpirited leaders had
withdrawn themfelves, or were fcattered far and
wide in different prifons ; the Republican principle, they contended, ftill remained *inviolate* and
incorruptible ! But where ? Not among the Nobles
who had ceafed to call Plebeian meetings, as the
latter fuppofed, to confult with them !—not among
the dependants upon thefe Nobles, who had feceded
from the Senate, and enhanced their crimes in
ceafing to harrafs the Minifter :—not among the
Commercial men in the City of London, whofe intereft it was to continue his fupport ; but it was to
France, that they ftill looked for the *fruits of the
Tree of Liberty*, which was to be yielded to them
alfo in due feafon. A fignal vi&ory, obtained by
the Auftrians, or any of the Allies, feldom damped
the hopes of Democracy ; this was looked upon, as
no more than the pruning of the branches, neceffary to make them fhoot again with frefh vigour.
If a commander was guilty, or accufed of corre-
fpondence with the enemy, he was only deemed a
canker-worm, who wanted to eat away the root.
If crowds of Emigrants or Priefts were adjudged
to death, it was ftill neceffary to deftroy them as fo
many locufts or caterpillars, who would have devoured the leaves ; or, if whole branches of this
precious

precious tree of liberty were carried away to en-
graft upon other trees in Italy, Egypt, or the In-
dies, ftill all was well; or, if the State Gar-
deners murdered each other, in confequence of
their difagreements about the manure, or the mode
of dreffing or fencing this hopeful fcion, ftill no
difference was made. Robefpierre, it was thought,
would certainly bring it to perfection. It was afterwards transferred to the Briffotines, the Sieyes,
and others, who continued to clip, and even ftunt
its branches; ftill, as the root was fuppofed to be
found and vigorous, and that it would again fhoot
out with all its energies, when the managers could
agree among themfelves, thefe retrenchments created no alarm. Every fucceeding Gardener, it was
prefumed, would mend the fault of his predeceffor;
and when it was put under the care of Bonaparte,
then was expectation, for a moment, wound up to
its higheft pitch; yet no fooner had his new plan
ripened into birth, than the falling off was inex-
preffible! Conjecture now feemed loft, and the
zig-zag flafhes of opinion, emitting a dark and du-
bious glare, refufed to be confined to any given
point. The multitude that fet out to follow the
French revolution, whatever courfe it might take,
though before fomewhat confufed by the many
languages it had fpoken, were now at their *ne plus
ultra*. They were exactly in the fituation of thofe
timid animals, who, preffed and perplexed by the
fhouts of the hunters, know not which courfe to
purfue. In fact, it was now neceffary, at all
events, to return; for as the Archimedean ground
of France, upon which all the world was to have
been moved, had vanifhed, and only prefented a
yawning gulph in its place—there was no alterna-
tive. And to thofe who had recovered their reafon,
in ever fo fmall a degree, it was now evident, that
the

the shelter still afforded by the British oak, was infinitely preferable to any exotic substitute whatever.

But independent of these facts, which no sophistry is able to palliate, and which no dexterity of movement can evade, the relative merits and demerits of Aristocracy and Democracy, I think, may be illustrated from some considerations not hitherto explored; and which, I presume, must place the weakness and insufficiency of the latter in a new point of view, and beyond all contradiction. To proceed; if we compare the ruling members of the body politic, to the superior faculties in the human frame, it will appear that there is a natural correspondence, and apposite relation between the lowest and worst passions in individual existence, and the tumultuous motions, the furor, or the panic fears of democracy in the great world, or organized society; while Aristocracy, from its stability, and the superior enlargement of its views, naturally approximates to Reason, and the cardinal virtues of Prudence, Justice, Temperance, and Fortitude; and thus, abstractedly considered, is, in fact, the *wisdom* and *maturity* of human society, in opposition *to its rashness, its youth, and inexperience.*

For an experimental conviction of the evanescency, and absolute nullity of a Democratic form of government, we need not look at France, where it has recently withered even in the hands of philosophers, but turn our eyes to the petulancy and littlenesses, frequently attendant upon parochial administrations; and for no other reason, but because the administrators are chosen as it were *by lot, out of the body of the people.* These annual rulers, when vested with a " little brief authority," are often so much elated by the sudden change, that the consequence they assume, not being *educated* to rule, nor
habituated

habituated to command, is such, as to render themselves perfectly ridiculous or contemptible; to say nothing of their too frequent acts of inhumanity, which have so often called for the interference of superior courts, more enlightened, and consequently more humane judges. Thus, if the proceedings of the committee-rooms had been as public as those of the bench, the sarcasm of the comic muse would have found an ample subject in their discussions and awards.

If we reduce the experiments of Democracy to a narrower circle, notwithstanding some of its advocates have told us, that the head of the government should resemble the president of a common-club, not *hereditary*, but removeable at the pleasure of the members, the *sovereign people*, we shall still find the theory at war with the practice. Let us examine the internal economy of the numerous popular societies under the name of benefit clubs: Are they not subject to perpetual squabbles, growing, as it were, out of the facility of crimination? Are not their concerns generally managed by a small junto, and their disputes generally settled by the clerk? No member is he, but only a servant to the society: yet to his opinion the majority mostly pay a deference, merely on the supposition of his superior abilities! Is not some one, in these cases, the indispensible character who must temper their acrimony, soothe their jealousies, and mitigate their awards? These are undeniable facts. A governing Democracy then, even in miniature, is a non-entity which can have no permanent existence but upon paper, or in the imaginations of those who mingle and confound theories for tried facts.

But, after all, if any thing is wanting to satisfy speculatists, who hold a contrary opinion, let them try

try Democracy upon their own families, and they will there find it the proper parent of mifrule and perpetual difcord. And as I have fhewn it to be that, in a conftitution, which the paffions are in the human frame, Ariftocracy is, and muft be, the *Reafon of a State*. As fuch, it poffeffes the indefeafible right of pre-eminence. I do not fay it can exift independently of Democracy; it has as much need of the ftrength and enthufiafm of the people, as they have of its prudence and ftability. But as the paffions in an individual fhould ever be fubfervient to reafon, it is equally juft, that the paffions of a nation fhould be conftantly fubjected to the controul of the more noble and fuperior faculties of the body politic.

If the late degeneracy of the French nation, into the madnefs of Democracy, has given us juft caufe of alarm for our domeftic tranquillity, its fubfequent approximation, under the prefent Grand Conful, towards that Ariftocracy we have juft fketched out, fhould allay every apprehenfion upon that fcore.

The points of refemblance, in the fituation of various branches of fociety, and the interefts of clafhing parties in this country, are not likely, after what has paffed, to fall into a fimilar direction with thofe of France, immediately preceding the late revolution. Even the difaffected, with the failure of eight years of experiment full in their faces, and the confequent degradation of the French revolutionary fpirit, are deprived both of precept and example. They are, in a manner, bound hand and foot, and thrown into the gulph of doubt and uncertainty. To recover from the fhock, therefore, which the centre of *all revolutions* has fuftained, muft be a work of time; and, before the public mind can be roufed into action, it will rather require

quire a fecurity againft future fufferings, than an indemnity for the paft.

In fine, the confequences of the French revolution may, for a long period to come, prefent themfelves at the elbow of every projeƈt for political change or innovation ; being perpetuated in thofe outrages of feeling, which cannot foon be forgotten, they are impreffed upon the minds of men, in charaƈters which cannot eafily be erafed. On the other hand, thefe charaƈters may even defy the power of obliteration, being too deeply indented in the earth, in the graves which have been dug for the millions who have fallen.

But though, all through the courfe of this work, I have infifted upon the impotence of the Democratic and Infidel focieties, unconneƈted with higher influence, or external agency; and though their meetings are no more holden ; ftill, as fcattered individuals, they are fufficiently numerous to do confiderable mifchief ; the Atheiftical clafs in particular feem moftly incorrigible. Incredible as it may appear, they are all looking forward for a millennium of their own ! And, notwithftanding the repeated failures of the French philofophers and revolutionifts, the Englifh Atheifts blindly infift, " that civil fociety is in a progreffive ftate of im-
" provement, to which every government, by its
" weaknefs and crimes, is unavoidably contribu-
" ting ; the final end of which, will be the diffolu-
" tion of them all ; and that the time is faft ap-
" proaching, and will infallibly arrive, when man
" and nature will be perfeƈt in all their relations,
" and the former will be able to live without go-
" vernment, without laws, and without fubmif-
" fion !!!" In England, thefe fanatics call themfelves the difciples of Mirabaud and Godwin. Upon the German Continent, one of their moft

notorious

notorious leaders is Profeſſor Fichte, late of the Univerſity of Jena; for a particular account of whom, *vide* Appendix to Vol. IV. of the Anti-Jacobin Magazine, and the German Journals for 1799, one of which, thus ſtrikingly contraſts the unexampled audacity of the new impiety, in an Epigram from the words of David—" *The fool hath* " *ſaid in his heart*"—

> The ancient Atheiſt, dreading to impart
> His impious creed, conceal'd it in his heart;
> But modern Atheiſts, fearleſs of the rod,
> In words and deeds, proclaim, " There is no God!"

Being warned, in ſacred writ, of theſe ſcoffers, that were to appear in the laſt times, we know, from the ſame authority, that their end is deſtruction, and that their folly ſhall be manifeſt to all.

But though, in a moral view, the anti-religious opinions of Infidels muſt meet with accumulated contempt from the Chriſtian world at large; yet, as thoſe who entertain them are all, without exception, tinged with revolutionary politics, and naturally deteſt every eſtabliſhment, the utmoſt caution continues neceſſary on the part of government, to prevent any combuſtion or real grievance, of which theſe incorrigible members might avail themſelves, to involve the community, as agents, in the proſecution of their invidious deſigns.

THE END.

Books and Pamphlets lately *publifhed* by JOHN HATCHARD, *Bookfeller* to HER MAJESTY, *No.* 173, *Piccadilly*.

A NARRATIVE of what paffed at Killalla, in the County of Mayo, and the Parts adjacent, during the French Invafion, in the Summer of 1798; attributed to have been written by the Lord Bifhop of *Killalla*. Price 3*s.* 6*d.*

Forethoughts on the General Pacification of Europe. Price 2*s.*

The Britifh Mercury; or, Hiftorical Tracts and Critical Views of the prefent Time; publifhed every Fortnight. Each Number 2*s.*

Two Sermons by the Lord Bifhop of Killaloe; one on the General Thankfgiving, November 29, 1798; and the other preached at the Chapel of Trinity-College, Dublin, April 7, 1799. Price 1*s.* 6*d.*

A Propofal for uniting the Kingdoms of Great Britain and Ireland, firft written in the Year 1751; attributed to the late Lord *Downfhire*. Price 1*s.* 6*d.*

Elements of Chriftian philofophy, by the Lord Bifhop of *Lincoln*, 2 vol. Price 14*s.*

Hiftory of the Interpreter of Prophecy; or, a View of Scriptural Prophecies, &c. &c. by *Henry Kett*, B. D. 2 vol. Price 12*s.*

An Appendix to the " Guide to the Church," in Letters to Sir Richard Hill, Bart. by the Rev. *Charles Daubeney*, LL. B. 2 vol. Price 10*s.*

Reports of the Society for Bettering the Condition of the Poor, &c. vol. 1, in boards. Price 6*s.* 6*d.*

Ditto, in Twelves. Price 2*s.*

Ditto, Seventh, Eighth, Ninth, Tenth, Eleventh, and Twelfth Reports, each 1*s.*

The Cheap Repofitory Tracts—the genuine corrected Edition, by Mrs. *H. More*, 3 vol.   Price 12s.

A Brief Examination into the Increafe of the Revenue, Commerce, and Manufactures, of Great Britain, from 1792 to 1799, by *George Rofe*, Efq. 7th Edition, with an Introduction, containing a Statement of the Revenue to the 10th of October, 1799. Price 2s.

Information to Overfeers; earneftly recommended to the Perufal of Overfeers, and all Perfons concerned in the Management of Poor-Houfes.   Price 6d. or 4s. per Dozen.

A Sermon, preached before the Lords Spiritual and Temporal, on Wednefday, February 27, 1799, 2d Edition, by the Lord Bifhop of *Durham*.   Price 1s. 6d.

Reflections on the political State of Society at the Commencement of the Year 1800, by John Bowles, Efq.   Price 3s. 6d.

The Progrefs of the Pilgrim *Good Intent* in Jacobinical Times, neatly printed in duodecimo.   Price 3s. 6d.

Practical Obfervations on the Revelation of St. John, written in the Year 1775, by the late Mrs. Bowdler, neatly printed in crown octavo.   Price 5s.

Poems and Effays by the late Mifs Bowdler, to which is now added an Effay on the Duties and Advantages of Sicknefs, beautifully printed, and an elegant Engraving of the Author.   Price, in boards, 1l. 1s.

Extract from an Account of certain poor Perfons in London, who cannot pay their *Income-Tax*, with Obfervations, and a Plan for their Relief, &c.   Price 1s.

Dearnefs occafioned by Scarcity, not Monopoly; a Sermon delivered in a Parifh-Church, in Northampton, on the General Faft, 1800; to which is added, an Appendix, containing Hints for the Improving the Condition of the Poor, together with a Table of the Average Price of Wheat in each Year, from 1595 to 1798 inclufive.   Price 1s. 6d.

JAMES WATSON

A MEMOIR

OF THE DAYS OF THE FIGHT FOR A FREE PRESS
IN ENGLAND AND OF THE AGITATION FOR THE
PEOPLE'S CHARTER

BY

W. J. LINTON.

And ever honour'd for his worthinesse.
CHAUCER'S KNIGHT.

MANCHESTER:
ABEL HEYWOOD AND SON, OLDHAM STREET.

To
ELEANOR BYERLEY WATSON
      her husband's true helpmate
  I dedicate
      this insufficient record of his life :
     W. J. LINTON.

New-Haven, U.S.A.
  1879

James Watson

Whoever rightly advocates the good of some thereby promotes the good of the whole.

JOHN WOOLMAN.

JAMES WATSON.

Inter vitæ, scelerisque purus.

M Y STORY is not of crowned Emperor or King, nor of any laurelled conqueror, the slaughterer of his fellow-men; it is not of One pre-ëminent, whether in the art of war or the arts of peace. I have to speak of only a plain man, indeed a true servant of Humanity, yet unintroduced by History to Fame, but whom nevertheless I will take as an examplar of some qualities for which we Englishmen pride ourselves,—wholesomeness and integrity of nature, stedfastness in purpose, firmness of will, indomitable courage, with power of endurance, and self-devotion:—a man whose life displayed at once the healthful sturdiness of the antlered oak, and therewithal such gentlest beauty of disposition as knightliest Sidney had rejoiced to know, and loved. Are such men rare? I trow not. But this man it was my happiness to know, as friend knows friend.

Concerning him, in some forgotten journal, with the date of March 30, 1833, I find the lines here following: his own writing:—

"TO THE HONOURABLE THE COMMONS OF THE UNITED KINGDOM OF GREAT BRITAIN AND IRELAND IN PARLIAMENT ASSEMBLED:

The Petition of James Watson, of 33, Windmill Street, Finsbury Square, in the County of Middlesex, Bookseller, Printer, and Publisher, at present unjustly confined in the New Prison, Clerkenwell:—

Showeth.—That your Petitioner is imprisoned in default of payment of a penalty of £20, having been convicted (under the 60th Geo. III., cap. 9) for selling for one penny a printed paper called the Poor Man's Guardian, containing "news, intelligence, and occurrences," not having a four-penny stamp affixed to it. Your Petitioner is therefore a debtor to the Crown for the sum of £20.

" Your Petitioner intreats the consideration of your Honourable House to the very severe punishment inflicted upon your Petitioner by the magistrates of the Bow Street Police Office, Sir Frederick Roe and Thomas Halls, Esquire, by whom your Petitioner was summarily convicted in a penalty of £20, and, in default of payment, subjected to six months imprisonment, without the intervention of a trial by jury.

" Your Petitioner is the more surprised at this injustice, for in all previous proceedings for similar offences, on the first conviction, no individual received, at the utmost, more than three months imprisonment.

" Your Petitioner also informs your Honourable House, that, in the honest discharge of his business as a general bookseller, your Petitioner exposed for constant sale, not less than twenty different periodicals, at the price of one penny: among others—the Penny Magazine, the Penny Cyclopædia, the Saturday Magazine, the Christian's Magazine, the Working Man's Friend, &c., some of which pamphlets are under the patronage of the Lord Chancellor and others of the King's present ministers, and the Bishops of the Church of England, as by Law established: and for the sale of which weekly papers the publishers and proprietors have never received any molestation; though the magistrates have admitted that all these publications equally violate the Act under which your Petitioner has been convicted, and which demonstrates that it is the opinions advocated in the Poor Man's Guardian that the Commissioners of Stamps, and the Government, are anxious to suppress, and not the protection of the revenue against the loss it is said to sustain from the circulation of cheap political papers.

"In proof of this statement, your Petitioner begs leave to point out to your Honourable House, that an information was laid at Bow Street, against the publishers of the Literary Gazette, and although the number of the publication then before the Magistrates contained twenty-one articles of news, the proceedings were quashed, on the plea that no other persons but the Commissioners of Stamps or their agents could lay informations against offenders; since which period the publishers have proceeded unmolested, and in open violation of the Act, with the perfect knowledge of the Commissioners of Stamps.

"Your Petitioner claims the attention of your Honourable House, to the fact of your Petitioner being subjected to the same treatment in this prison as pickpockets, swindlers, passers of bad money, committers of rapes and other criminal acts of a like kind, to the great pain and annoyance of your Petitioner, and in violation of an Act 4th Geo. IV., cap. 64, entitled 'an Act for consolidating and amending the laws relating to the building, repairing, and *regulating*, of certain Gaols and Houses of Correction in England and Wales,'—which Act states that arrangements shall be made to preserve the health, and improve *the morals of the prisoners*, and in another part of the same Act of Parliament it is expressly prohibited to class persons for offences like that of your Petitioner with the abandoned characters, and crimes before mentioned.

"Your Petitioner has a separate sleeping-cell, of small dimensions, usually appropriated to the solitary confinement of refractory prisoners; to which cell your Petitioner occasionally resorted during the day, to write a note, or read a book, and to escape from the mental torment of hearing from his associates the most horrid swearing and the grossest licentiousness. Yet even this self-inflicted solitude has been denied your Petitioner, by one of the visiting magistrates of the prison, named Samuel Hoare, banker, of Lombard Street, he having strictly prohibited all access to the cell during the day.

"Your Petitioner having to intermix with so many prisoners, the number in the ward varying from 20 to 60, is in constant dread of contracting disease or of being infested with vermin. Your Petitioner is also constantly exposed to the severity of the weather, there being but one fire for the use of all the prisoners confined in the ward. Your Petitioner has complained to the visiting magistrates of the cruel treatment to which he is subjected, but without obtaining any redress.

"Your Petitioner, therefore, appeals to your Honourable House to institute an inquiry into these complaints and to redress the abuses which subject him to the treatment of a criminal ; or to take such steps as your Honourable House, in its wisdom, may consider best to cause the immediate discharge of your Petitioner from his cruel and unmerited imprisonment.

"And your Petitioner will ever pray."

To which, before going farther, I would append these Words of a Believer (the Abbé Lamennais) :—

When you see a man led to prison, or to punishment, say not in your haste—This is some wicked man who has committed a crime against his fellows !

For peradventure it is a good man who has wished to serve his fellows, and who for that is punished by their oppressors.

The inscription here-beneath is, or not long since was, on the base of a statue erected in 1831 on a little plot of railed-in garden ground, in Burton Crescent, London.

JOHN CARTWRIGHT,

born 28th Sept., 1740; died 23rd Sept., 1824;

THE FIRM, CONSISTENT, AND PERSEVERING ADVOCATE OF UNIVERSAL SUFFRAGE, EQUAL REPRESENTATION, VOTE BY BALLOT, AND ANNUAL PARLIAMENTS.

It was the eve of the "Reform Bill," passed in 1832 by the Whigs under the leadership of Earl Grey, an ancient professor of Major Cartwright's faith. Not that in office the Party attempted to carry out their earlier principles. Content with a £10 household qualification for electors in boroughs, and a leasehold, or a copyhold, qualification for electors in counties, they gave to the middle classes a privileged share in the government of the Country, to the exclusion of the mass of "the people": so enabling the middle classes to dictate laws after the shopkeeper's heart,— to wit, the Poor Law Amendment Act to check "the growing evil of pauperism," and the Repeal of the Corn Laws—for assurance of freër trade in labour.

Nearly two hundred years had passed since the religious and patriotic uprising of the English Puritans, since the day on which a number of " long

heavy swords with the initials *O.C.* on their hilts"
arrived at a certain farmhouse in Huntingdonshire,—
nearly two hundred years since the impaneling of
the grandest jury the world has known, for the
trial of a King. Exactly two hundred years since
Cromwell entered upon his St. Ives farm, to watch
and wait events. As yet Thomas Carlyle had
not spoken to remind Englishmen what manner of
man this Cromwell was. Even Godwin had not
understood him. Universal England had forgotten
him: or recalled him only through her established
church services, the lustral commemoration of the
Blessed Martyrdom and the more galling annual
thanksgiving for the unhappy Restoration of The
Dissolute,— those two most religious ceremonies
which, as was well remarked by Walter Savage
Landor, had been perfectly satisfactory had each
been but transferred to the other occasion. The
race of the Puritans had passed away. The occu-
piers and tillers of the soil grew loyal on their stint
of bread per week; hand-loom weavers upon Yorkshire moors had their occasional cut of the Roast
Beef of Old England from cows dying with dysentery;
and the Factory System, that crowning mercy of the
Trader's Reign, had already begun to indicate its
capacity for degrading and deteriorating our mechanics. From underground, in coal or iron mines,
as yet was no report. Mankind knew nothing of
the women and little children buried living there.

Priestley's house, in the very heart of England,
Shakspere's own neighbourhood, had been burned
by a Church-and-King mob, Priestly fleeing for his
life to America; as Paine also, for daring to assert
the Rights of Man.   Peterloo had given proof that
the yeomanry (ignorant farmers and farmers' sons)
could be trusted to ride down insurgent peasants
(blood for bread); and the gentle hanging and dis-
emboweling of the Cato Street conspirators* (part of
the coronation ceremonies at the accession of George
the fourth) was a fair sample of the tender mercy of
the Crown.   In truth the French Revolution with its
fierce assertion of human right had thoroughly scared
the lords and gentlemen and clergy and all that was
pious and respectable in the kingdom; and woe to
him who dared but whisper a hope of political or
religious liberty!   Paine spoke, and was expatriated,
outlawed, vilified.   Let the serf keep silence!   The
infamous Castlereagh Cabinet (Castlereagh committed suicide in 1822) had stamped the legend of
Tyranny on our coinage ; and none other might pass
current.

> " Corpses are cold in the tomb,
>   Stones on the pavement are dumb,
>   Abortions are dead in the womb ;
> And their mothers look pale, like the white shore
>   Of Albion free no more.

* Conspirators by contrivance of the Government.   The conspiracy
was concocted by a Government Spy.   No uncommon proceeding
with monarchical governments ; and done, it is said, for the sake of
example.

> " Her sons are as stones in the way ;
> They are masses of senseless clay ;
> They are trodden and move not away :
> The abortion with which she travaileth
> Is Liberty smitten to death." *

Smitten to death, and even lament forbidden! Among
other devices, to confine the people in that ignorance
in which is the supposed security for a brutish sub-
mission, was a tax of four-pence on every periodical
publication wherein political events were chronicled
or discussed: or in legal phraseology,—" which contained news, intelligence, or occurrences, or remarks
or observations thereupon, or on matters in Church
or State."   In days when the cost of a single letter
(postage between London and Bristol one shilling)
put it beyond the reach of the day-labourer (nine
shillings a week "good wages" for a man with a
family of nine†) this tax was equivalent to a prohibi-
tion: it was so intended.   By which means, with the
additional precaution of fore-given security, required
of the printer or publisher, as provision for penalties
to be imposed by the Government for whatsoever

---

* " *Lines written during the execrable Castlereagh Administration*,"
by Percy Bysshe Shelley.

† In the agricultural districts.   And for mechanics: date March,
1833 :—"WILLIAM CARTER, Journeyman Framework-knitter, of
Leicester: his average labour seventeen hours a day, his earnings
nine shillings a week, subject to the following deductions : Frame-
rent, 1s. 3d.; Winding, 4d.; Candles, 9d.; Needles, 3d.; Master's
charge on work, 3d.; Coals for the shop, 3d.; Seaming, 10d.;
leaving 5s. 1d. for house-rent, fuel, soap for washing, food, and
clothing, for himself, a wife, and five children."

writing they might choose to call offensive, political knowledge was, so far as governmental wit could devise, confined to the respectable classes, whose interests were said to consist with the perpetuation of helotry. Chained (the chain of the modern slave is hunger), chained and gagged, what was to be done toward enfranchising the masses?

By two ways only can Liberty be won : by the sword, or by the power of the spoken or the written word.

By the sword? The well-born, whose fathers fought with Cromwell, now, lame with gout and their brains all muddled by thick port, were at the side of tyranny ; and where, among the perennially clammed, was to be found an arm fit to wield the flail of the Lord and of Gideon? Brought up and stunted in the upas-shadow of a Church drunken and disreputable, in the words of Cowper—

"a priesthood such as Baal's was of old,"

the untaught albeit repeatedly catechised populace were the blind tools as well as victims of oppression; or took refuge in the passive discontentedness of such aped puritanism as was inaugurated by Wesley, which looked to heaven for reward of its surly patience and no more had care or thought for the establishment of God's Laws on earth. By the sword? And where the swordsmen, the "strong-limbed and godly men who dare"? The strong

earning rheumatism at the plough, the godliest
skulking in some conventicle, cursing prelacy, but
cursing equally the "infidel" disturber of that
"order" in which prelacy grew rank.   One bravely
spoken word had been heard in England since the
Rascal Restoration: he who spoke it,—I repeat, and
will have again to repeat his name—THOMAS PAINE,
has to this day obtained as little grace or honour
from the lips of dissenting presbyters as from the
rounder mouths of priests or popes.   Who else has
been so violently assailed, whose character so vil-
lainously abused?   Church-legal and dissent have
rivaled each other in slanderous vituperation against
the wretch who would have broken the double chain
of clerical and political imposture.   They made his
name a bye-word and a reproach, and set a mark on
whosoever was known but to have read his writings.
Yet men kept those writings hidden away, as their
fathers had kept the first English Bible.   And read,
but were too weak to act.   For the mass, not only
were they weak, but from their souls was washed out
("by the blood of the Lamb," in the jargon of the
herdsmen) even the wish for rebellion.   Pig-like,
worse than sheepish, they grunted around their
troughs, listened or did not listen to the Te-Deums
of the swineherds; and in due season were gathered
to their fathers—in the smoke-room.   Thicker dark-
ness than wrapped old Egypt plagued by Moses
swathed anarchic England in those days.   A few

alone,* like Cartwright, from time to time ventured
to repeat the first principles of government; and
whoso could might read the hand-writing on the
wall: else no glint of light was visible in the gloom
save some sparks of the fire which France had
kindled, scattered by the hand of Paine.   One
Richard Carlile (not Thomas Carlyle nor of his
kindred) thought it were well to keep some heat alive
by republication of Paine's works.   One William
Carpenter looked for a chance of redemption through
the mediation of a free and untaxed press.   Rebels,
but not men of war, they believed in the might of
the Word, which sometimes is able to prevent the
Sword; and hoped, for themselves and their fellows,
to vindicate that first of all liberties, the Miltonic
liberty "to know, to utter, and to argue freely according to conscience."   Single-handed each began
to put his thought into action.   With them to will
was to do.   Give them honour for so much!   Not
all men are so brave.

Of Carlile, on account of his connection with
Watson, there is need to say something more.
Carlile began his work in the day of a crazy king, a
profligate regent, and a corrupt government, 1817.
The son of a shoe-maker, he was born in 1790 at

---

* Among them not to be forgotten Benjamin Flower, the Editor of
the *Cambridge Intelligencer*, with his profound reverence for woman-
hood, the father of two of the most beautiful and most gifted and
influential women in England,—Eliza Flower, the musical composer,
and Sarah, author of *Vivia Perpetua, Hymns*, &c., the wife of W.
Bridges Adams.

Ashburton in Devonshire. As a boy he collected
faggots to burn in effigy " Tom Paine," the "Guy
Fawkes" of that time. Apprenticed to a tin-plate-
worker (Bunyan was also a tin-man), he followed
that business until his twenty-sixth year, when,
meeting with Paine's works, he was converted, and
moved to eke out scant employment by the sale of
Cobbett's *Register*, Wooler's *Black Dwarf*, and other
"radical" periodicals which the authorities were
anxious to suppress; none of which, however, he
thought bold enough. Some success as a vendor led
him to publish on his own account; first Paine's
political and afterwards his theological writings. He
brought out too Southey's *Wat Tyler*, when the poet
turned conservative would have suppressed it, selling
of it twenty-five thousand copies; also Hone's
Parodies, if every one else was afraid to meddle with
them; parodies on the Church Services, which cost
him eighteen weeks of prison pending the trial of
Hone, whose acquittal released him. Later,
however, in November 1819, he was sentenced, as a
publisher of " blasphemous and seditious libels," to
suffer three years imprisonment in Dorchester jail,
with a fine of £1,500. In his defence he read to the
Court the whole of Paine's *Age of Reason*, and
outwitted his preventers by printing the whole in a
cheap form as part of the report of the trial—a
privileged publication. In February, 1821, his wife
was imprisoned; and later in the same year his
sister also. Nevertheless the sale of his publications

went on, volunteers helping, until it was judged necessary to form a " Constitutional Association " with the name of Arthur Duke of Wellington heading a list of subscribers, to provide funds, to defend State and Church by the vigorous prosecution of Carlile's shop-men and assistants. Susanna Wright, William Holmes, George Beer, John Barkley, Humphrey Boyle, William Tunbridge, Joseph Rhodes, James Watson, and others, so prosecuted, suffered terms of imprisonment, from six months to three years. Some samples of the sentences may as well be given here.

JOSEPH RHODES: for selling a " blasphemous " pamphlet, two years in the House of Correction, with hard labour, and sureties for £500, for good behaviour *during life*.

WILLIAM CAMPION: for *Age of Reason*, three years in Newgate, and his own bail in £100 to keep the peace for life.

JOHN CLARKE: for selling Carlile's *Republican*, three years in Newgate, and to give bail for good conduct during life.

W. V. HOLMES: two years in prison; there told that " if hard labour was not expressed in his sentence, it was implied."

HUMPHREY BOYLE: in prison for five months before his trial, eighteen months afterwards, had a mind, my lord ! " that can bear such a sentence with fortitude."

WILLIAM TUNBRIDGE: for Palmer's *Principles of
Nature*, in prison for two years, fined £100, "to
be imprisoned until the fine be paid."

So dealt the Law with those offenders. But they
tired out the "Constitutional Association," and the
Law itself began to limp. So much, without more
particulars, may suffice to show the conditions of free
thought and free speech in that day of "Bible-and-
Unicorn" supremacy; to show also the dauntless
temper of Carlile, whose full service of incarceration
for the public liberties extended to *nine years and four
months*. Before his last sentence, anticipating his
being punished by a fine, to be paid—if he would
pay it at all—only out of the continued sale of his
prohibited publications, and that he might also be
required to find sureties for future lawful behaviour,
he gave in the following deposition :—

"—And deponent saith that, in case the Court
should think a penalty necessary, this deponent has
no other property from which he can pay a fine than
[his] printed books; and from the political business
in which this deponent is involved he can not
reasonably ask any other persons to become sureties
that his future proceedings may not be construed
into a political offence; not but that this deponent is
anxious to live in peace and amity with all men,
but that there do exist many political and moral
evils which this deponent will through life labour to
abate."

Watson's petition to the " Commons " has date of
1833. Twenty-one years later, no fortune made, nor
sought—his business was not money-making, but
health needing rest, and a bare sufficiency for
life to be expected from the continued sale of his
publications even in hands less energetic,—his
retirement from business gives occasion for friends to
gather round him, to express esteem and gratitude,
with presentation of some formal address to be kept
as a reminder of their appreciation of his worth.
Acknowledging the address, he rendered account of
his career. I will not interrupt; his own modest
words, as reported with some approach to accuracy,
will stand for prologue and sufficiently as text for
farther speech.

" I was born in an obscure town, Malton in Yorkshire, in the year 1799. Our family consisted of my
mother, my sister, and myself, my father having died
when I wanted about a fortnight of a year old; so
that I had but one parent to do the duty of two, and
I am proud to say that duty was performed with all
a mother's kindness and devotion. My mother,
although poor, was intelligent, as a proof of which I
may state that she was a teacher in one of the
Sunday-schools of the town. To my mother I owe

my taste for reading and what school education I
received. I could read well, write indifferently, and
had a very imperfect knowledge of arithmetic. At
twelve years of age a clergyman, in whose family my
mother had lived before her marriage, and who paid
for the last three or four quarters of my schooling,
induced my mother to bind me to him as an
apprentice for seven years, to learn field labour,
work in the garden, clean horses, milk cows, and
wait at table; occupations not very favourable to
mental development. At that time there were no
cheap books, no cheap newspapers or periodicals, no
Mechanics' Institutions to facilitate the acquisition
of knowledge. The government was then in the
hands of the clergy and aristocracy, the people,
ignorant and debased, taking no part in politics,
except once in seven years, when the elections were
scenes of degradation and corruption. During my
stay with the clergyman my mother again became a
servant in the family, and well do I remember
reading by the kitchen fire during the long winter
nights. My favourite books were two folio volumes
with illustrations, one a history of Europe, the other
a history of England. My interest in those books
was intense, and many times I thought, while poring
over them, shall I ever see any of the places here
described? and I have seen many of those places
since, although my position then seemed so
unfavourable. At the end of six years my master's

wife died, and he retired into Nottinghamshire, which caused my indentures to be cancelled. After this I lived with my mother and sister; but, not liking to be a burthen on them, myself and a companion, similarly situated, resolved to quit our native town and seek employment (and some relatives) in Leeds. We succeeded in finding both. I found employment at a drysalter's as warehouseman, and had the charge of a saddle-horse.

" It was in the autumn of 1818 that I first became acquainted with politics and theology. Passing along Briggate one evening, I saw at the corner of Union Court a bill, which stated that the Radical Reformers held their meetings in a room in that court. Curiosity prompted me to go and hear what was going on. I found them reading Wooler's *Black Dwarf*, Carlile's *Republican*, and Cobbett's *Register*. I remembered my mother being in the habit of reading Cobbett's *Register*, and saying she wondered people spoke so much against it ; she saw nothing bad in it, but she saw a great many good things in it. After hearing it read in the meeting room, I was of my mother's opinion.

" In that room I first became acquainted with one who became my friend and constant companion ; his name was William Driver. His name and my own were spoken of together amongst our friends in the same manner as afterward my name was

mentioned with that of my friend Hetherington.
From this time until 1822 I was actively engaged
with Mr. Brayshaw, Joseph Hurtley, Robert Byerley
(my wife's father), Humphrey Boyle, Mr. Gill, and a
number of other friends, in collecting subscriptions
for Mr. Carlile, spreading the liberal and free-thinking
literature, and, by meetings and discussions,
endeavouring to obtain the right of free discussion.
In 1821 the Government renewed the prosecutions
for blasphemy, and Mr. Carlile (then in Dorchester
gaol under a three years sentence) appealed to the
friends in the country to serve in the shop.
Humphrey Boyle was the first volunteer from Leeds.
He was arrested, tried, and sentenced to eighteen
months imprisonment. On the 18th of September,
1822, I arrived in London, the second Leeds
volunteer. I served in the shop at 5, Water Lane,
Fleet Street, until Christmas, when I spent a week
with Mr. Carlile in Dorchester gaol. At that time
Mrs. Carlile and Mr. Carlile's sister were his fellow-
prisoners. We talked over many plans and business
arrangements.

" At this time the plan of selling the books by a
sort of clockwork, so that the seller was not seen,
was in practice. Notwithstanding that precaution,
Wm. Tunbridge was arrested, tried, and sentenced to
two years imprisonment, and fined £100. In
January, 1823, Mr. Carlile took a shop in the Strand,
No. 201. Mrs. Carlile, having completed her two

years imprisonment, resided in the rooms above the shop. Towards the end of February I was arrested for selling a copy of Palmer's *Principles of Nature*, taken to Bow Street, and, not able to procure bail in London, was sent to Clerkenwell prison, where I remained six weeks. Two of my Leeds friends, Joseph Hurtley and Robert Byerley, then became bail for me. My trial took place on the 23rd of April, at Hick's Hall, Clerkenwell Green, before Mr. Const and the bench of magistrates. I conducted my own defence. Reports had been circulated that the persons who had been taken from Mr. Carlile's shop were but tools in the hands of others, and incapable of defending themselves: which was not true, as Boyle and others of the shopmen had defended themselves.

" In my defence I endeavoured to prove from the Bible that Palmer was justified in what he had written, when I was interrupted, and told that I " might quote from the Bible, but not comment upon it." I was convicted, and sentenced to twelve months imprisonment in Coldbath-Fields prison, and to find bail for my good behaviour for two years.

" I had for fellow-prisoners Wm. Tunbridge and Mrs. S. Wright. Mr. Tunbridge and I had a room to ourselves. During this twelve-month I read with deep interest and much profit Gibbon's *Decline and Fall of the Roman Empire*, Hume's *History of England*, and other standard works, amongst others Mosheim's

Ecclesiastical History. The reading of that book would have made me a free-thinker if I had not been one before. I endeavoured to make the best use of the opportunity for study and investigation, and the more I read and learned the more I felt my own deficiency. So the twelve months confinement was not lost upon me. Mr. Tunbridge did not share my studies. The evenings I usually spent with another fellow prisoner (Mr. Humphrey), an intelligent man, who possessed a good collection of books. For three or four hours after dark we read to each other, after which until bedtime we conversed or played a game at cribbage. We found the governor, Mr. Vickery, an old Bow Street officer, a kind-hearted man, more disposed to multiply our comforts than to restrict them. And thus our prison life passed as pleasantly and profitably as was possible under the circumstances. I was liberated on the 24th April, 1824, and shortly after visited Malton, to convince my mother and friends that imprisonment had not made me a worse son or a bad citizen. In May, 1824, the Government renewed the prosecutions of Mr. Carlile's assistants, by arresting, trying, and convicting Wm. Campion, John Clarke, T. R. Perry, R. Hassell, and several others, some of whom were sentenced to three years imprisonment.

" After visiting Leeds, and the friends there, I returned to London. I applied for employment at a number of places, but found my having been in prison, and shopman to Mr. Carlile, a formidable difficulty, and I incurred in consequence considerable privation. I had, however, a townsman and school-fellow in London, whose bed and purse were ever at my service. That friend, I have the pleasure to say, is now present.

"In August of this year, Mr. Boyle, who had managed Mr. Carlile's business sometime, withdrew from it, and I was applied to by Mr. Carlile to supply his place. I conducted the business from that time until Mr. Carlile's liberation from Dorchester gaol, in November, 1825.

"At the end of 1825 I learned the art of a com-positor, in the office in which Mr. Carlile's *Republican* was printed. Whilst there I was attacked by cholera, which terminated in typhus and brain fever. I owe my life to the late Julian Hibbert. He took me from my lodgings to his own house at Kentish Town, nursed me and doctored me for eight weeks, and made a man of me again. After my recovery Mr. Hibbert got a printing press put up in his house, and employed me in composing, under his directions, two volumes, one in Greek, the other in Greek and Eng-lish. I was thus employed from the latter part of 1826 to the end of March, 1828. In 1825 I was first introduced, by my friend Mr. Thomas Hooper, to the advocates of Mr. Owen's New Views of Society; and to the end of 1829 I was actively engaged, helping to form co-operative associations and societies for

political and religious liberty. In April, 1828, I
undertook the agency of the Co-operative Store at
36, Red Lion Square, and I remained in that employment until Christmas, 1829.

"In the beginning of 1830 I visited Leeds, Halifax, Dewsbury, Bradford, Huddersfield, Todmorden,
Wakefield, and other places, to advocate the establishment of co-operative associations. In May I took
the house 33, Windmill Street, Finsbury Square, and
there commenced the business of bookseller. During
the excitement occasioned by the French Revolution
in July I took an active part in the numerous
enthusiastic meetings following that event.

"In 1831 I became a printer and publisher. My
friend Julian Hibbert gave me his press and types.
The first use I made of them was to print Volney's
Lectures on History, which I composed and printed
with my own hands. At this time I became a member of the National Union of the Working Classes.

"In 1832 the excitement of the people on the subject of the Reform Bill was at its height. The
cholera being very bad all over the country, the
Government, to please the Agnewites, ordered a
'general fast.' The members of the National Union,
to mark their contempt for such an order, determined
to have a procession through the streets of London,
and afterwards to have a general feast. In April I
was arrested, with Messrs. Lovett and Benbow, for
advising and leading the procession. We were

liberated on bail, tried on the 16th of May, each conducting his own defence, and all acquitted. Towards the end of this year Mr. Hetherington was sentenced to his second six months confinement, in Clerkenwell prison, for the *Poor Man's Guardian.*

"In February, 1833, I was summoned to Bow Street for selling a *Poor Man's Guardian.* Before the magistrates I justified my conduct in selling unstamped newspapers. They considered me as bad as my friend Hetherington, and sentenced me to six months in the same Clerkenwell prison. I was liberated on the 29th July, and attended the same day a meeting to commemorate the third anniversary of the French Revolution, in which Mr. Julian Hibbert, the Rev. Robert Taylor, Mr. Hetherington, and others, took part. At the end of this year I was engaged with Mr. Saull, Mr. Prout, Mr. Franks, and Mr. Mordan in fitting up the Hall of Science, in the City Road, as a lecture room for Rowland Detrosier. In January, 1834, occurred the lamented death of Mr. Julian Hibbert. In his will he again gave me a marked token of his regard, by a legacy of 450 guineas. With this sum I enlarged my printing operations. My legacy was soon absorbed in printing Mirabaud's *System of Nature*, Volney's *Ruins*, Frances Wright's *Popular Lectures*, Paine's *Works*, and others. In addition to the legacy, I incurred a debt of £500 in printing and publishing these. In April I took part in the great meeting of the Trades Unions in

Copenhagen Fields, in favour of the Dorchester labourers.

" On the 3rd of June, 1834, I was married. Before a month was over I was again summoned to Bow Street, but preferred a short trip to Jersey, where I stayed three weeks. On the 7th of August the officers again seized me, and I was taken to Clerkenwell for my third imprisonment. I was liberated on the 21st of January, 1835, and from that time to the present have remained unmolested. In 1836, '37, '38, I was engaged with others in the formation of Working Men's Associations, and assisted to prepare the document called the People's Charter. In 1840 took place the trial of Henry Hetherington, for ' blasphemy.' He was convicted and imprisoned. My friend honoured me by dedicating his trial to me, and I have been more proud of his testimony and friendship than of anything I ever received. Since 1841 my bookselling and public work is known to most of my hearers.

" . . I have trespassed on your forbearance : but I had one object in view,— to show my fellow-workmen that the humblest may render effectual aid to the cause of progress if he bring to the task honest determination and unfaltering perseverance."

The two great questions to which the life of Watson was devoted were the right of free speech and free printing, and the right of every man yet unconvicted of disabling crime to take part in choos-

ing the nation's government. Or, to speak more
exactly, the single question with him was the eleva-
tion of his own class (that of the workman—the man
dependent on his work for daily bread) by these
means :—not without thought of the education to be
obtained even through the struggle for them. Of the
man himself and of what he encountered his own
words have told us. Some additional notice I would
give here of his work ; first of what he did for the
establishment of a free press. I have no complete
list ; but I find the following among his publications :—

> Paine's Works, complete. *   [Also issued separately]
> The Life of Paine.
> Mirabaud's System of Nature.
> Palmer's Principles of Nature.
> Volney's Lectures on History ; and Ruins of Empires.
> Sir W. Drummond's Preface to the Œdipus Judaicus.
> Byron's Cain ; and Vision of Judgment.
> Shelley's Queen Mab, with the prosecuted Notes.
>   . . . Masque of Anarchy.
> Clark's Letters to Dr. Adam Clarke,—on the Life and
>   Miracles of Christ.
> Robert Owen's Essays on the Formation of Character.
>   Lectures : Evils of Existing State of Society.
> Robert Dale Owen : Discussions with Origen Bacheler
>   on the authenticity of the Bible, and on the
>   existence of God.

* Including the *Address on the Abolition of Royalty*. Translated
from the French, in Brissot's *Patriote Francais* of 27 October, 1792 ;
unknown in any previous English version. It first appeared,
placarded by Achille Duchatelet, on the walls of Paris, on occasion
of the King's flight. The first demand for the Republic.

Frances Wright d'Arusmont's Lectures.
. . . .   A Few Days in Athens.
Buonarotti's History of Babeuf's Conspiracy.
Godwin's Political Justice.
Lamenois' Modern Slavery.

Other works mostly of the English *Index*—marked for
expurgation or legal physicking out, not without risk
he kept on sale; but those named above were all, I
believe, produced at his own cost, many set up and
printed by his own hands, the legacy from Hibbert
his only capital. Most of these works were unprofitable; he but asked if a book ought to be read instead
of prohibited, would it be useful to his class; then he
calculated how cheaply it could be brought out,
content if all his business returns were sufficient for
the simplest necessaries of life and to enable him to
publish more. The Society for the Diffusion of
Useful Knowledge, with harlequin Brougham at
their head, and funds and interest without stint, did
not show such a list. Their notion of useful
knowledge included neither political nor religious,
certainly excluded both subjects, except when cooked
for the occasion, as were Harriet Martineau's
untruthful Poor-Law Tales. *

*Poor-Laws and Paupers illustrated, 1833-4. Harriet Martineau, as
it seems to me, has not been quite understood. Instead of being an
exact writer, she was in matters of fact most inexact. Her famous
Poor-Law Tales, got up to order, to prepare the way for the inhuman
Whig "Poor-Law Amendment" Act, are clever romances. She
could not wilfully misrepresent, but she gives half-truths, which most
often are worse than lies. How much of this was owing to her

And as to social questions—I do not hesitate to assert, the daring of one earnest man did more for the education of the People in those days than all that easy issue of Whig benevolence, all that kindly supply of juiceless chaff for the troughs or mangers of the " insatiable wild beasts," [a parliamentary term for the populace,] whom they hope so to tame to run more quietly in harness.

In some respects, also, to Watson and to his fellows is owing whatever good came from his rivals : for neither the Diffusion Society's *Penny Magazine* nor its follower the Christian-promoting *Saturday*, with other " Information for the People " (Chambers'—to wit), had perhaps appeared but for the sake of counteracting the influence of the new cheap literature of Watson and Hetherington, Cleave, Heywood, and others. Like the Whig Political Union (not "national," but only of the middle classes), a new middle-class literature had to be encouraged, opportunity for profit of

---

imperfect hearing, how much rather to one-sidedness of brain, it might be hard to say. But the same want of exactitude is noticeable even in a book in which there is barely possibility of personal bias ; her *Guide to the Lake Country*, the district in which she lived. Having so to speak of her writings, I am bound also to add my full recognition of the manly integrity of her life ; her desire for truth and her stedfast adherence to whatever she thought to be true. She was a feminine Cobbett, sturdy, somewhat antagonistic, honest, well-meaning, but hasty in judgment and expression ; notwithstanding all her manliness with the woman's weakness of argument and impulsiveness of assertion.

course duly considered also, lest the malaria from the low lands should infect the healthy dwellers in Respectability, and the comfortable continuance of " Things-as-they-are " be even more influentially vexed by outcries for alteration. So much can the one man win for his age. So much can be done by so little leaven of earnestness.

I have said Watson cared rather than for profit to place good reading before the uneducated people : wherefore he was content with the smallest margin of gain enough for means of life. But he cared also for the correctness and decent appearance of his books, even the cheapest. They were his children (he had none else): he would have them well-dressed and fit to be admitted anywhere. You may tell a man's character by everything he does : this man's was to be seen in a penny pamphlet. Good matter, carefully edited, on fair paper, cleanly printed, squarely folded, thoroughly stitched, in plain but always neat binding or wrapper : you could not but see that it was done by a conscientious worker, gifted with a keen sense of fitness and propriety. He set his face against the proverb " cheap and nasty," desiring to break down the prejudice of his time (not yet quite obsolete) which confounded radicalism with coarseness and dirt ; sometimes did not lack at least an outer justification. There was no mistaking an edition by J. Watson. To him life and all its circumstances were to be kept in wholesomeness, though means of beautifying might fail him. The pride of the poor man was his. His honesty should be clean-skinned and pure, if his clothes were thread-bare ; his public appearance as his home ever dignified, made worthy of respect. Serving in his shop, he had pleasant and informing words for all who sought his wares ; the character of this or that book, about which you asked, might be trusted to his judgment. His conversation, if you cared to make acquaintance with it, supplemented what he sold : what he had given—if apostles in his day had been able to print and live without debt. Of debt he had a horror. If in his stead [in later days], at the receipt of custom you found his wife, you could be sure that he was either at press work or otherwise employed toward new desired or needed publication, or attending to some public duty—in deputation somewhere, in open meeting, or in prison for his honest, unspared service in the working-man's behalf. In prison he used his leisure for self-instruction ; he had no other University experiences. Out of prison he was one to whom the strivers for the Miltonic liberty of speech looked for counsel of sound judgment, and for that certainty whereon to lean which is the prerogative of the most manly—the stay of fibre that can not yield, nor flinch. He was of the stuff [nearly sold out—I hear— a not-paying manufacture] of those old martyrs, who smiled when they were flayed alive— [our modern nerves tremble as we read of agonies they bore]—

who thrust their hands into fire to pluck out un-
harmed their more tender souls. For the respect in
which his probity and his business qualities were
held, his name as treasurer of subscriptions in aid of
political sufferers may be voucher enough. He was
one to whom you might have trusted untold gold :
he *could* not have wronged you of the smallest coin.

I have been able to give some statement of his
doings as publisher; of his public work there is
neither record nor possibility of adequate recollection.
Here confining myself to the endeavour for free
publishing, and for the extension of liberal opinions,
his books indicate but one direction of his energies.
In class meetings, in public meetings, he was as
earnest : no man else more earnest. Only his friend
Henry Hetherington was more zealous. But
Hetherington would neglect his own business rather
than the public duty should be left undone, and so
was ruined and incurred reproach; and Watson,
wiser, in his home more happily aided, tempered zeal
with discretion and neglected nothing : not even the
" mint and anise." Not the slightest duty unfulfilled
marred the perfectness of his harmonious life. Yet
he never failed his friend : and by their side, as
prudently active, constant, intrepid, and devoted, as
Watson himself, stood Richard Moore, to whom and
Dobson Collet—the energetic secretary of the
" Society for the abolition of the Taxes upon
Knowledge " we mainly owe their ultimate repeal in

England, the remission of that last, worst penny, as
it was justly called, which the shifty Whigs retained
when, forced by the publications and exertions of
Hetherington and his friends to give up their *four-
penny* stamp, they hoped by continuing the lesser but
no less offensive hinderance to be still able to crush
the cheap newspapers : beaver-like biting off what
might (but did not) divert the hunters, to save their
miserable lives ; ready ever, as foretold of them by
Job [or were there Whigs in his time ?] to give all
else, even to their dirty skins. Am I unjust to these
English Girondists ? Sir Henry Bulwer answers for
me. " The Whig Party was—always essentially an
exclusive party : *its regards were concentrated on a clique*,
to whom all without it were tools and instruments."
The mantle of Castlereagh had fallen on them, and
they prophesied in right Tory fashion : Woe to a
discontented People !

In the history of the fight for free newspapers—
any record more complete than is room for in this
personal memoir, Hetherington rather than Watson
will be recognised as the real leader ; Watson himself
so placed him. When, in 1831, the law-administrators
declared that any endeavour to give political
knowledge to the people was *ipso facto* to be considered
illegal, and as such worthy of punishment,
Hetherington came forward to contest their ruling,
by the publication of his *Poor Man's Guardian*, "a
weekly paper for the People, established contrary to

'Law' [afterwards published in defiance of "Law"],
to try the power of Might against Right : * which will
contain [in the words of the prohibitory Act, here in
italic] *news, intelligence,* and *occurrences,* and *remarks and
observations thereon,* and *on matters in Church and State,
tending* decidedly *to excite hatred and contempt of the
Government and Constitution* of the tyranny *of this Country
as by Law established* and also *to vilify* the ABUSES of
religion; and will be *printed in the United Kingdom for
sale, and published periodically* (every Saturday) *at
intervals not exceeding twenty-six days;* and will *not exceed
two sheets;* and will be published *for a less sum than sixpence* (*to wit,* the sum of ONE PENNY); *exclusive of the
duty imposed by the* 38 *Geo. III cap* 78 *and* 60 *Geo. III c.*
9, or any other acts whatsoever, and despite the
'laws,' or the will and pleasure, of any tyrant or body
of tyrants whatsoever, any thing herein-before or anywhere else contained to the contrary notwithstanding."

Repeatedly convicted, hunted like a wild beast,
imprisoned, stripped of his property, he gallantly
maintained the contest to a successful ending : till he

* Before this he had brought out daily, and then weekly,' *Penny
Letters to the People, by the Poor Man's Guardian,* acting upon a
suggestion by Carpenter, who proposed so to evade the stringency of
Castlereagh's Act. The first of these *Letters* was issued in October,
1830; but on his being convicted of illegality he changed the title to
the POOR MAN'S GUARDIAN, in bold and open defiance. The first
number with this heading is dated 9 July, 1831. The *Guardian* was
at first edited by Edward Mayhew; and after his untimely death, by
James Bronterre O'Brien.

forced his opponents to abandon that straining of the
Law in which the magistracy had been their handy
tool, and to bring him, June the seventeenth, 1834,
to fair trial by a jury.

The result is told under the heading of the
number of the *Guardian* for June 21 :—

"This paper, after sustaining a Government
prosecution of three years and a half duration, in
which UPWARDS OF FIVE HUNDRED PERSONS* were
unjustly imprisoned, and cruelly treated, for vending
it, *was on the trial of an ex officio information filed by the
Attorney-General against Henry Hetherington, in the Court
of Exchequer before Lord Lyndhurst and a special jury,
declared to be a strictly legal publication.*"

* One of the imprisoned and cruelly treated, as his own story has
told us, was Watson. Not in opposition, but in aid of the common
cause, he too published a weekly paper, similar to the *Guardian*,—
the *Working-Man's Friend*, which escaped prosecution, the fiercer
assailant perhaps drawing off the government fire.

Among these sufferers for the Liberty of the Press ABEL
HEYWOOD is not to be left unnoticed. He was wholesale agent in
Manchester for the *Guardian*, and a tair target for prosecution. He
took his prison degree, paid his fines when he could afford it, and
went on selling his *Guardians*. Then the Authorities seized the
papers in the hands of the carriers, and various devices had to be
sought in order that they might pass in safety. Some packed with
shoes, some in chests of tea, some otherwise, they sent the proscribed
goods through the country; and their circulation continued until the
reduction of the duty, as was expected, ruined the cheap papers. By
this time the *Guardian* had been made the foundation of a business;
which Heywood's perseverance and ability enlarged until he,
denounced in earlier days as seditious and a blasphemer, became a
"well-to-do" citizen, and the honoured Mayor of Manchester.

HETHERINGTON was born in London in 1792 ; and
brought up as a printer.   He was one of the earliest
and most active of working-men engaged with Dr.
Birkbeck in founding the first Mechanics' Institute ;
and in 1830 he was chosen by the radical working-
men of London to draw up a plan for Trades Unions,
which became the basis of the National Union of the
Working Classes, out of which sprang the movement
for the People's Charter.

For four years he bore the brunt of the battle for
a free Press.   Ever busy in the interest of his class
during the Whig Reform ferment, he was among the
most zealous as well as of the wisest leaders of Chartism afterwards.   A ready speaker, bold and fluent,
passionate, sarcastic, or humorous on occasion [he
had a spice of fun in him through all his trouble], he
was deservedly popular in those days ; and in the
Chartist Convention of 1839 sat as delegate from
Stockport and for London.   Time and thought, and
toil also, he gave unsparingly in aid of the social and
religious thriving of the time.   He closed his unrest-
ing and useful life, after a few days' sickness, on the
24th of August, 1849.   For his character, I find no
better words than some I wrote to be spoken at his
burial.   There is not a word I would retract or modify.

[Of all the men in the battle for the People's Right,
I have known none more single-minded, few so
brave, so generous, so gallant as he.   He was the
most chivalrous of all our party.   He could neglect

his own interests (which is by no means a virtue, but there is never lack of rebukers for all failings of that kind), but he never did, and never could, neglect his duty to the cause he had embraced, to the principles he had avowed. There was no notoriety-hunting in him: as, indeed, so mean a passion has no place in any true man. And he was of the truest. He would toil in any unnoticeable good work for freedom, in any "forlorn hope," or even, when he saw that justice was with them, for men who were not of his party, as cheerfully and vigorously as most other men will labour for money or fame or respectability. He was a real man, one of that select and "glorious company" of those who are completely in earnest. His principles were not kept in the pocket of a Sunday coat (I don't know that he always had a Sunday change of any sort): but were to him the daily light which led his steps. If strife and wrath lay in his path, it was seldom from any fault of his; for though hasty, as a man of impulsive nature, and chafed by some afflictions, he was not intolerant, nor quarrelsome, nor vindictive. Men who did not know him have called him violent. He was, as said before, hasty and impetuous, but utterly without malice; and he would not have harmed his worst enemy, though, in truth, he heartily detested tyranny and tyrants. Peace be with him, on the other side of this fitful dream which we call life; peace, which he seldom knew here, though his nature was kindly and his

hope strong, though he loved Truth, and wilfully
injured no man. One of the truest and bravest of
the warm-hearted has lain down among the tombs,
not worn out, but sorely wearied. May we rest as
honourably, with as few specks to come between our
lives and the grateful recollections of those who have
journeyed with us. If our young men, in the vigour of
their youth, will be but as enthusiastic and as
untiring as was Hetherington even in the last days
of his long exertion, we need not despair of Freedom,
nor of a worthy monument to a noble life, which else
would seem but as a vainly-spoken word, wasted and
forgotten.

Yet again, peace be with him; and in his place
the copy and thankful remembrance of the worth we
loved in him.]

So much I have had to say of Hetherington, not
only as his due—but too scantily rendered, but also
because for twenty years he was the tried and trusty
comrade of my friend. What Hetherington did was
ever seconded by Watson: what Watson did had
surely Hetherington's endorsement. One can not be
praised but the other will "divide his crown." In
Watson's own words, spoken at his friend's grave,
their "single friendship never knew two interests."
During the struggles of the Unstamped they were as
David and Jonathan: the two were as one. That
battle gained, they stood in as close brotherhood in
preparation and in action for the People's Charter.

Hetherington's victory was decisive. The pursuit was left to Moore and Collet. Prosecution was at an end. The logical conclusion required no longer defiance, but persistence only; and the secretary of the Society for the removal of the yet remaining penny, C. Dobson Collet, might be fitly surnamed the Persistent. And Moore——I must halt yet somewhile in my memoir of Watson, not to neglect his other friend and comrade, dear to him as Hetherington, yet closer than he,—my own friend also, RICHARD MOORE.

Born in 1810, he was brought up as a wood-carver, in which art he excelled. Early in association with Lovett, Hetherington, and Watson, he shared all their labours; and marrying a niece of Watson, a wife worthy to be so mated, became yet more intimate with him. For forty years he was among the foremost in all the liberal movements of the time. One of the framers of the People's Charter, he sat in the first Chartist Convention; he was a leading elector in the radical borough of Finsbury; he was active in behalf of Poland and of Italy. But most especially he claims remembrance as chairman [Collet, as already said, secretary], during thirteen years, of the Society for the Repeal of the Taxes on Knowledge, the main promoter of that unceasing agitation which forced the Government to give up not only the stamp, but also the taxes on advertisements

and paper. Ever labouring with remarkable single-
ness of purpose in the public service, he was as
modest as active. Few men—says one who knew
him well—" have enjoyed the confidence and
friendship of leading politicians more than he. All
the prominent English Radicals and liberal Exiles he
could reckon among his friends.   The purity of
his life was only equalled by his disinterestedness.
There was something singularly earnest, gentle, and
chivalrous, in his character." I can only echo these
words, knowing how well they were deserved. To
him—if the claim of the Wife had not been paramount
—this memoir would have been dedicated; him I had
ever in my mind while writing, him first among those
for whose approval of my work I cared. True-hearted
man and sterling patriot! no name could be more
fitly coupled with your friend's. Only since com-
pleting my record of him I learn that in death as in
life you are together.   Richard Moore died December
7, 1878.

Here too, before I leave the story of the Unstamped,
may be fit place to render homage to JULIAN HIBBERT,
treasurer, and " chief prop " of the Victim Fund
during the battle for the *Guardian*.   There is his life.
In his will, out of regard to his relatives, people of
"family," his mother (I believe) a catholic, he ordered
his papers to be destroyed and forbade his friends to
speak of him.   " I ask only silence."   So passed into

oblivion one more of the martyr myriad, the ransom
for Humanity. His friends could not but respect his
prayer. It is now too late to inquire concerning him.
He died in 1834.

His portrait is marvellously like Shelley's. He
seems indeed (that I learned) to have been a prose
Shelley, with the same gentleness of nature and chivalrous zeal against Wrong; like Shelley also in his
public spirit, in his generosity, his tenderness of disposition, his poetic enthusiasm for what he deemed
the Right.

Free publication of honest thought and fair opportunity for sharing in the national government : these
two most important of all questions moved, as I have
said before, the life of Watson. The second made
him a " Chartist." That Chartist phase of English
history has been misunderstood or misrepresented by
party writers of the time, and seems now almost ob-
literated from the minds of the present generation of
"liberal" politicians, who do not even dream how
much they are indebted to it. On this account, as
well as because of its important influence on the life
of England, some words beyond the relation of
Watson's actual part in it may not be out place.

The movement for the " People's Charter," as
already told, grew out of a document prepared by
Hetherington in 1831, in which originated the *National
Union of the Working Classes*, "to collect and organise a
peaceful expression of public opinion," for "protection of workmen in the free disposal of their labour,"
to obtain an "effectual reform in Parliament" (instead of the unfair arrangement projected by the
Whigs), "the repeal of all bad laws, and the enactment of a wise and comprehensive code." The association was formed after the model of Wesleyanism :
class-leaders being appointed at general meetings to
groups of from thirty to forty members, the classes

held weekly at members' homes. Those meetings were for political instruction, by readings and discussions. In what records remain of the proceedings I trace Watson's name, not prominent (he never cared to be prominent) but honourably conspicuous. The declaration of principles was drawn up by him and Lovett.

NATIONAL UNION OF THE WORKING CLASSES.

" *We, the Working Classes of London*, declare—

" 1—All property (honestly acquired) to be sacred and inviolable.

" 2—That all men are born equally free, and have certain natural and inalienable rights.

"3—That governments ought to be founded on those rights; and all laws instituted for the *common benefit* in the protection and security of *all the people :* and not for the particular emolument or advantage of any single man, family, or set of men.

" 4—That all hereditary distinctions of birth are unnatural, and opposed to the equal rights of man; and therefore ought to be abolished.

" 5—That every man of the age of twenty-one years, of sound mind, and not tainted by crime, has a right, either by himself or his representative, to a free voice in determining the nature of the laws, the necessity for public contributions, the appropriation of them, their amount, mode of assessment, and duration.

"6—That in order to secure the unbiassed choice of

proper persons for representatives, the mode of voting
should be *by ballot;* that intellectual fitness and moral
worth, *and not property*, should be the qualification for
representatives; and that the duration of Parliament
should be but for *one year.*

"7—We declare these principles to be essential to
our protection as working men, and the only sure
guarantees for the securing to us the proceeds of our
labour, and that we will never be satisfied with the
enactment of any law or laws which do not recognize
the rights enumerated in this declaration."

The declaration headed a call for a public meeting
of the "useful classes, to be held in the space in
front of White-Conduit House, London, on Monday,
November 7, 1831, at one o'clock precisely, for the
purpose of solemnly ratifying" the above principles.
The Whig Government met this popular challenge by
the formation of a counter association, the "National
Political Union" of the middle classes, to support, by
force if necessary, their class Reform Bill, and to
prevent anything beyond that. The meeting of the
working-men was prohibited by Lord Melbourne;
special constables were mustered; troops were
marched in; and orders were given to arrest every
member of the Committee of the Association who
should appear at the place of meeting. The temper
of those Reformers—Grey, Russell, Brougham, etc.—
may be sufficiently indicated by this: the Whig Press

at that very time daily threatening the Tories with revolution, boasting of a hundred and fifty thousand men armed to enforce their partial measure. I read in the journals of same date, of four poor men in Lancashire sentenced, under an obsolete and forgotten law, to twelve months imprisonment for *unlawfully assembling on a Sunday evening*. But they were not assembled for worship of the Reform Bill.

The Association was wise enough not to accept this provocation to a conflict undesired and which could but result in useless bloodshed: it gave up the meeting, and went on its peaceful way. In May of the next year a second attempt at public meeting, preparatory to calling a National Convention, was put down by actual force: the police attacked the assembled people. In the melèe a policeman was killed, stabbed by a man whom he had struck. The jury upon the coroner's inquest returned a verdict of "justifiable homicide," on the ground that no proclamation forbade the meeting, that the Riot Act was not read requiring the crowd to disperse, and that "the conduct of the police was ferocious, brutal, and unprovoked." This, at least in intention a fit pendant to the Tory massacre at Peterloo, is what is known as the Calthorpe-Street affair, having happened on some open ground thereby. Care was taken as soon afterwards as possible to build upon the land, effectually to prevent other meetings there.

The National Union did good educational work;

but had to give way to the consolidated Trade-
Unions, then as now standing, as they always must
stand, as obstacles to political endeavour : tempting
men with better wages for to-day from what in moments of despondency seems the hopelessness of going
to the root of the evil. Still, staunch to their principles, the originators and leaders of the Union made
another attempt for the wiser action by the formation in 1836 of the London Working Men's Association,* whose published addresses earned a warm
meed of praise, for all his dainty literary taste and
careless poet dislike of political strife, from "the
gentlest of the wise," Leigh Hunt. To that association too belongs the honour of sending an Address to
the foreigner,† the first public attempt to exorcize the
king-fostered spirit of national antagonism.

In February, 1837, the Association, having prepared their way, convened a public meeting at and
within the Crown-and Anchor tavern, in the Strand
(indoor meetings not illegal then), at which a petition

---

* In a list of those who took most active part in the association I
note the names of Henry Hetherington, James Watson, William
Lovett, Richard Moore, William Moore, John Cleave, Henry Vincent,
Robert Hartwell, Henry Mitchell, William Savage, Charles H.
Neesom, Thomas Ireland, S. Calderara, George Julian Harney :
names to be ever held in grateful remembrance by English working-
men.

† An Address to the Working Classes of Belgium, I believe drawn
up by Lovett, on occasion of the imprisonment of one Jacob Katz,
for calling a public meeting of workmen to discuss their grievances.

to the House of Commons, for universal suffrage and
new ordering of Parliament, obtained the signatures of
three thousand persons. This petition the Association left in the hands of Mr. Roebuck for presentation;
and toward his support requested a conference with
those members of the reformed House who professed
liberal principles. Eight came: T. Perronet Thomp-
son, Joseph Hume, Charles Hindley, Daniel O'Connell,
Dr. Bowring, John Temple Leader, William Sharman
Crawford, Benjamin Hawes. The conference took
up two nights, the members of the Commons' House,
except Hawes, assenting generally to the principles
in discussion, but most of them hesitating as to any
immediate promotion of the same. O'Connell dodged,
he would have substituted an ingenious scheme of his
own; failing which, he agreed with the course of the
Association,—not honestly intending, as afterwards
sufficiently appeared. The following resolutions were
adopted: June 7, 1837.

1—We agree to support any proposition for Universal
   Suffrage made on the Petition emanating from the
   Working Men's Association, when presented to the
   House of Commons by Mr. Roebuck.

   Proposed by Daniel O'Connell.
   Seconded by Charles Hindley.

2—We agree to support and vote for a Bill or Bills,
   to be brought into the House of Commons, embodying the principles of Universal Suffrage, Equal

Representation, Free Selection of Representatives without reference to Property, the Ballot, and Short Parliaments of fixed duration, the limit not to exceed three years.

Proposed by Daniel O'Connell.
Seconded by Charles Hindley.

3—We agree to support and vote for a Bill, or Bills, to be brought into the House of Commons, for such a reform in the House of Lords as shall render it responsible to the People.

Proposed by Daniel O'Connell.
Seconded by Sharman Crawford.

4—That a Committee of twelve persons be appointed, to draw up a Bill, or Bills, in a legal form, embodying the principles agreed to, and that they be submitted to another meeting of the liberal members of Parliament and the Working Men's Association: that the following be the persons appointed—

DANIEL O'CONNELL	HY. HETHERINGTON
JOHN ARTHUR ROEBUCK	JOHN CLEAVE
JOHN TEMPLE LEADER	JAMES WATSON
CHARLES HINDLEY	RICHARD MOORE
T. PERRONET THOMPSON	WILLIAM LOVETT
W. SHARMAN CRAWFORD	HENRY VINCENT

Proposed by J. Temple Leader.
Seconded by Robert Hartwell.

The labour of drafting the bill was deputed to Roebuck and Lovett; but, owing to Roebuck's parliamentary and other engagements, fell almost wholly on Lovett. Every clause was carefully considered in the Association, and the bill so completed finally submitted to the public, as THE PEOPLE'S CHARTER— "*the outline of an Act* to provide for the just representation of the People of Great Britain and Ireland in the Commons' House of Parliament: embracing the principles of *Universal Suffrage, No Property Qualification* (for Members), *Annual Parliaments, Equal Representaticn, Payment of Members,* and *Vote by Ballot.*"

On the 6th of August, 1838, at a meeting at New-Hall Hill, Birmingham, the People's Charter was formally approved, even, after some reluctance, by the Household Suffragists of the Birmingham Political Union. From this time Feargus O'Connor also joined the Chartists. At this meeting it was proposed that a Convention of the Working Classes should be summoned, and a National Petition be obtained, and that a National Rent should be collected to defray the necessary expenses. On the 17th of the following September, another meeting in the Palace Yard, Westminster, the High Bailiff in the chair, solemnly adopted the People's Charter and National Petition, and recommended meetings throughout the country to appoint the delegates "to watch over the Charter and Petition when presented to Parliament." At this meeting one of the resolutions was moved by Ebenezer Elliott, "the Corn Law Rhymer."

The delegates so appointed met, on February the

4th, at the British Coffee House, as the *General Convention of the Working Classes*. The Convention, 55 members, was elected by show of hands of, it was said, three millions of persons: " 450,000 had been assembled for the election on Kersal Moor, 200,000 at Peep-Green, 250,000 at Birmingham, 200,000 at Glasgow, etc." Enthusiasm ran high; money was subscribed; meetings were multiplied; the Convention sent out its members as missionaries through the country; Chartist Associations sprang up in the manufacturing districts, and elsewere. On the 13th of May, the Convention, having deposited the petition of 1,280,000 persons with Mr. Attwood, transferred their sittings, for the consideration of "ulterior measures," to Birmingham; and then dispersed to hold simultaneous meetings throughout the country. The Petition was presented to the "Commons" on the 14th of June, and on the 12th of July 235 members, against 46, refused to consider its prayer. Meanwhile the Whig Ministers had not been forgetful of their old tactics, the foolish conduct of some members of the Convention playing into their hands. Threats of what the people could do were lightly used; whereupon some sections of them began to arm and train themselves: ill-founded reports of the war-like determination of the masses were given in to and published by the Convention; which moreover had neither forelooking purpose, nor unanimity, nor capacity for guidance. Arrests were made, for training and drilling;

arrests of members of the Convention for " seditious "
speaking. The Calthorpe Street policy was renewed,
and a band of London Police, ordered down to Birmingham, while the Convention was sitting there,
attacked the people peaceably meeting in the Bull-
Ring. Lovett, the secretary of the Convention, was
arrested for signing an address justifying the resistance of the people. And when the Convention met
again in London with very reduced numbers, on the
10th of July, it was but to see their petition mocked
at ; to decide on the 16th of July, upon a "sacred
month "—an abstinence from all work for that period,
to begin on the 12th of August throughout the
country, for the overthrow of the Government ; and
to substitute, on the 5th of August, one day's holiday
for the impracticable month, and to appeal to the un-
political Trades, to help a manifestation then. On
the 14th of September the Convention dissolved,
having utterly failed in everything, except the
Petition.

The baseless reports of Chartist power and determination still continued, over-living even the deplorable contradiction furnished by Frost's abortive
attempt on Newport, on the 4th of November: an
attempt induced by a too-ready credence to bragging
exaggerations of others. On the 26th of December a
second Convention met in London, with the object
of saving Frost and his fellow-victims. But the game
was up. All that remained was the popularity of the

ever-active O'Connor and of his *Northern Star* : both
of which should have been turned to account.

Lovett, having come out of prison, founded in
1842 the " National Association," to re-commence a
general organization.   He was joined by most of
those who had been most active in the Working
Men's Association ; and violently opposed by
O'Connor and his party,—a party which had been
helped by the *Star* to keep up the agitation since
1839, but which had changed Chartism to O'Con-
norism and almost lost sight of the suffrage while
looking for allotments of unprofitable land.   But
Lovett was impracticable ; and his new association,
after obtaining a few hundred members, dwindled
into a debating club, and their hall became a dancing
academy, let occasionally for unobjectionable public
meetings.   Lukewarmness among the more sensible
of the working men, and aimless violence, not without
good intention, among the O'Connorites, just kept
alive the name of Chartism till the proclamation of
the French Republic, in February, 1848, awoke old
hopes in England.

Then again some efforts were made to resuscitate
the movement. Another National Convention met in
London, under the auspices of O'Connor, to super-
intend another Petition.   Almost every fault of the
first Convention was repeated.   Blustering talk led
to foolish riots. The Petition with " 5,700,000 signatures," afterwards reduced to 2,000,000, including

fictitious, was presented on the 10th of April; and on the 17th the Convention dissolved to meet again on the 1st of May, as a "National Assembly," to carry the Charter. But all was now confusion. Even the elections (by show of hands) without principle or method; 3,000 men electing three members for London, 100,000 at Halifax electing one. The Assembly simply exhibited its incapacity, and merged into the "National Charter Association," which pursued the same course: gathering tumultuous crowds of purposeless men, doing little to teach, and nothing to organize, unable even to command regular subscriptions, and mustering throughout the country only some 5,000 paying members after the ten years' turmoil. Those of the Chartists still anxious in 1848 to make some attempt at organization, found themselves joined by but a few hundreds, by them feebly, and for a little while. Men no longer rallied around the Chartist banner; some few only when it was dragged in the dirt. Chartism went down in the whirlpool of its own folly.

So much of the history of Chartism I wrote in 1851,* not sparing censure, having to warn the people

* *English Republic*, Vol. 1, Art. *Chartism.* In the same article I wrote—From first to last Chartism never had a real intention, that is a clear resolve *to act;* and consequently never made even an endeavour at such an organization as would be necessary for successful action. There was in the National Union of the Working Classes, and elsewhere, ordering for mutual instruction; there were not unfrequent efforts to broadcast political knowledge among the masses; there were well-tried arrangements for getting together so

against a repetition of their folly; for in that hour a
few were looking beyond the twilight dimness of a
parliamentary reform for the day-star of the Republic. Nevertheless, when you have consented to
the verdict, be not content to note the emptiness of
that Chartist hubbub, but take notice also that such
outspokenness, albeit over-loud for gentility or dis-
creeter ears, however vainly Jericho-like, was a true
and honest and manly utterance, healthier by far
than aimless grumbling or the secret conspiracies by
Castlereagh's provocation-and-spy system laid grub-
like in the hearts of justly discontented Englishmen.
Chartism had at least a manlier fibre. Also, under-
neath and beside all the blatancy were wiser thoughts
at work, not able indeed to lead that horn-mad mob
in triumph, but even in defeat preparing for future
conquest. The better temper of the oppressed, better
for all the bellowing, was due to Watson and
Hetherington, and their friends, and when the
trumpet-braying gave out, some memories of principles taught by them remained. It must also be
acknowledged that, although the Charter is not yet

---

many thousand throats to bawl—"The Charter! and no surrender!"
but there never was any serious endeavour to create and weld together
a popular power with a determined object, determined means for
obtaining it, and determination to act accordingly at whatever risk.
The elements of success were left out of view. Nothing else.

History, giving the meaning of Chartism, will say—It was the
outcry of a long-felt want [in 1819 Cartwright's petition had a
mil on signers], *a people's protest*. Nothing more or less than that.

law, the very noise scared those in high places, the
unhanged Hamans; and poor had been the likelihood
of the many changes and many and great improvements in England, in the action of its still usurping
legislature and in the condition of its yet unenfran-
chised people, but for the stirring and striving, so
liberally criticized and so satisfactorily condemned,
of those insatiable wild beasts, as comfortable
reformers suffered them to be called, who only asked
for their own rights (for rights not doubted by the
men who refused them), who neither harmed nor
wished harm to any, and whose worst follies were
their being from over-tameness themselves so easily
dismayed; and sometimes a blind rush, haply incited
for their own political ends by the party that drove
back and scourged them. To my Lords Melbourne,
Grey, and Russell, to such well-placed patriots as
Brougham, to Burdett and Hume and O'Connell, be
awarded the juster condemnation of History,—for
that, having betrayed the people, they stung them
designedly to madness, for the sake of their own
iniquities frustrating the hopes their own promises
had evoked. No fouler blot smirches our English
record than the conduct of the Great Whig Party
from 1830 to 1850; their treachery toward Freedom
culminating in the acceptance of the Napoleon-
Infamy. On the tomb of the Whigs one word is
epitaph: the name of a trickster: PALMERSTON. And
unless the Miltonic day must be excepted, the

glorious hours of Eliot, Cromwell and Vane, no
worthier cause has occupied the heart of England in
any time than that so unsuccessful struggle for a
" man-like place," the real and avowed object of the
framers of the PEOPLE'S CHARTER.

I am losing sight of Watson, as he, and
Hetherington too, was lost sight of in the whirl of the
O'Connor madness.   The demagogues led the
multitude by the ears, while the tyrants looked on,
grinning at the confusion, nor failed to stir the witch-
broth when it seemed to cool.   The old plan of
inciting in order to betray, rife in those horrible days
of Castlereagh and Sidmouth, and not forgotten
during the battle of the Unstamped, [sturdy old
Cobbett made the House of Commons see it when
their own Committee of Inquiry gazed through
Parliamentary spectacles in vain], was not left out of
the tactics of our Whigs succeeding to Tory place
and practice, although lack of practice caused their
sometimes untoward blundering: blunders of less
consequence when every man had to cook "his own
goose" and "the land to be bought up at £40 for an
acre" were the cries of the popular wool gatherers;
and the fleeces followed.

When O'Connor first and afterwards Ernest
Jones led their followers into that wilderness of land-
schemes, and the mill-owners, Cobden, Bright, & Co.,
sought to bribe the ill-fed masses with repeal of the
tax on bread (free trade was what they talked about—

intending nothing of the sort), wanting cheap bread
—the cheapest possible, that "our mills" might be
run at less cost, and poor-rates reduced to a minimum
—[I except those nearer angelic or poetic "free-
traders" ignorant of policies and earthly realities, who
were persuaded philanthropically to abet any belly-
filling schemes, good for at least an afternoon]—
Hetherington and Watson stood aside : not denying,
but even as strenuously affirming the usurpation of the
People's Land, nor heedless of the agony of the hungry
poor; but resolute in their wise perception and determination that before all things it is necessary for a
man to be a man, so recognised by the Law and by the
Custom of Society ; after which he may be strong
enough to vindicate other rights.   Never before :
though the aforesaid poets and good-meaning angels
sit in Parliament cheek by jowl with the wealthiest
free-traders, and are regularly allowed to speak, and
to vote—in the minority.

Feargus O'Connor and his minions [I believe in the
honest intentions of O'Connor, I think a truer man
than O'Connell, though of the same not-small-potato
breed] never faced the real Chartists—Hetherington,
Watson, Lovett ; while in Finsbury, the most radical
of metropolitan boroughs, where Moore and Watson
lived, represented by surgeon Wakley, stalwart editor
of the *Lancet*, and Thomas Slingsby Duncombe,* the

* The pluckiest on the Opposition bench ; an aristocrat by nature as
well as circumstance, yet ever on the people's side, as fearless as

Corn-law League dared not call a public meeting. Not that an opposing hand would have been raised in favour of the bread-tax, but that as from one voice, they would have heard the rebuke of their more selfish policy—Give us our place of manhood, and that with other injustices shall cease ; but manhood even before bread !

In the last attempt to inspire the Chartist body with a reasonable soul Watson stood first. One of the callers, and chairman, of the first meeting for con-gratulation of the French Republicans on their triumph in February, '48, he sought at once to rein-vigorate Chartism, toward a Republican party in

---

Roebuck and more popular, as Roebuck sided with the Whigs in their poor-law policy : a man to be honoured if only for his chivalrous conduct in the exposure of the infamous meddling with the Exiles' letters (Mazzini's and others') in 1844, in the English Post Office, when the Bandieras were betrayed to Austria, and Sir James Graham as whipping-boy for Lord Aberdeen got more than his share of the well-merited but insufficient punishment that followed that most rascally un-English proceeding. My own and Lovett's letters to Mazzini were among those opened. He and Watson were of the few public-spirited enough to characterize the conduct of the Government as it deserved. In the Commons' debate Shiel, Macaulay, and Wakley stood with Duncombe ; but the Liberal Party " would not embarrass" the Ministers. Even Milner Gibson excused himself from speaking : his head "too full of Muscovado sugar." And the Free Traders (some excepted, men such as W. J. Fox, Bridges Adams, old Francis Place, P. A. Taylor, and W. E. Higson, editor of the *Westminster Review*) were of course regardless of English honour.

England.* But the effort was too late. Habits of occasional enthusiasm and evaporation in blustering talk unfit the best-intentioned for sacrifice or work, and the earnest man had poor following. Five men such as Watson had been powerless for the revival of Chartism, self-slain.

* At our first meeting he was unanimously chosen president; but he gave way to Thomas Cooper (author of the *Purgatory of Suicides*), then just from prison, whose name he thought might be more useful.

I first became acquainted with Watson in, I think,
1835. I had been brought up more piously than the
Church of England requires; but the liberal tenden-
cies of my brother-in-law, Thomas Wade, the poet
(then editor of *Bell's New Weekly Messenger*, a semi-
radical London newspaper), some reading of Voltaire
and Shelley, and the stirring words of Lamennais in
his famous Scripture anathematised by the Pope*—
the *Paroles d'un Croyant*, had brought me in contact
with the religious and social and political problems
of the time. More especially I was indebted, through
occasional attendance at his lectures, to William
Johnson Fox, the sometime Unitarian minister, the
most eloquent orator of his day, the virtual founder
of that new school of English radicalism, which looked
beyond the established traditions of the French
Revolution, and, more poetical, escaped the narrow-
ness of Utilitarianism : a man wiser than his com-
peers, who but for lack of boldness (perhaps accounted
for by his physique) had been the royal leader of the
English democracy. So prepared I was ready for
active sympathy with the cause of the people, then
finding expression in the cry for political enfranchise-
ment. Almost every day I passed a certain book-shop,
a few doors from Bunhill Fields [The Dissenters'

* "We damn for ever this book of small size but huge depravity."
                                                        Pope Gregory XVI.

burial-ground : John Bunyan lay there,—but there
was a talk lately of building over it]; and often I
stopped to buy one of Roebuck's *Pamphlets* or Gilbert
A'Becket's *Figaro in London* (the forerunner of *Punch*),
Volney's *Ruins of Empires*, the *Lectures on History*, or
such-like ; sometimes remaining to talk with the shopkeeper, a thin, haggard, thoughtful man, with a grave
but gentle manner, who appeared more interested
than tradesmen usually are in the worth of what he
sold.   This was Watson, recently from prison, and
still suffering the effects of his imprisonment.

In 1838 I was projecting what I hoped might
become a sort of cheap library for the people : to
consist mainly of selected extracts from such prohibited
works as were beyond the purchasing-reach or time
for study of working-men ; and I had grown into so
much confidence in Watson that I went to him to
publish for me.   He laid before me the difficulties
in my way, the cost of money and of obloquy ; then,
finding me still resolute, offered to me (a nameless
stranger) his books and his services.   At the end of
six months, a volume of weekly numbers completed,
my means nearly used up, I reckoned with him.   The
account rendered, I noticed that there was no charge
for folding or stitching—some two thousand a week
—say fifty thousand sheets in all. He had been " sure
that the book could not pay," and he and his wife had
folded and stitched every copy, to save me so much
of expense.

So began our friendship,—a friendship for which, as for other such, I paid with the loss of early friends and home affections : for in those days (not fifty years ago) Deists were certainly Atheists ; Unitarians were not allowed to call themselves Christians ; and a good churchman of the established persuasion would disown his son, and the mother pass him in the street, unspoken to, for no better reason than that he refused to join publicly in their communion,—not from preference for any vicious pleasures (which would have been forgiven), but only because of conscientious scruples, inoffensively avowed, which rendered him liable to the name of Infidel. The man so treated was my friend. I speak of what I know. For Unitarians, they lived, married, and traded, among themselves : a proscribed class, though the worthiest of England's sons and daughters, and the foremost English thinkers, were of that sect. The friendship of one such as Watson was cheaply bought at the price.

For years after, working in the same cause, our course of public action one, our trust in each other unlimited, I familiar in his home and he always welcome in mine, we moved together in every endeavour of the time : his earlier friend Hetherington not closer to him, I believe, than I was. So I learned to know him thoroughly. If I speak here of myself, it is to warrant my speaking of him ; and I have a right to the honour his comradeship bestows upon me.

When Frost and his fellow-rebels, Zephaniah Williams and Jones, were condemned to death as leaders in that mad outbreak at Newport, brought about by the foolish bluster of O'Connor, it was in the little sitting-room behind Watson's shop that we copied out a petition for a reprieve, the subscriptions to which, in not many hours, became so numerous that the Government was fain, for all reluctance, to send a stay of the death-sentence (the punishment was afterwards commuted to transportation for life) to Hetherington's more prominent place of business, in the Strand, to be there exhibited in order to allay the popular excitement.

Later, in 1840 or '41, when the Government visited its political opponents, the working-class, with indictments for blasphemy (the pretext a mere sale, amongst other publications, of an intemperate book, Haslam's *Letters to the Clergy*, so pushed into notoriety), and Heywood, one of the prosecuted, advised retaliation upon the Government partisans, that goose and gander might be served with the same sauce, it was Watson, with Hetherington, who took up the case in London, by indicting four metropolitan booksellers of unimpeachable respectability for the same offence of blasphemy,—inasmuch as they had published or exposed for sale the " blasphemous and seditious " works of one Percy Bysshe Shelley, containing notably his *Queen Mab*, for which already, indeed many years before, William Clark

(if I mistake not the name) had incurred the vengeance of offended Law. We knew of course that
the book would but sell the more for prosecution;
we had no desire that it should be otherwise: but if
social disgrace from a conviction for "blasphemy"
was to be used as a weapon against us, it seemed
politic that, boomerang-like, it should return on its
employers. Conviction was sure: Law, like Physic,
always obedient to Precedent. Our purpose was to
prevent the trial of Hetherington,* or to affect his
sentence, if condemned. The first object was defeated: the indicted parties getting their trials removed from the Old-Bailey sessions to the higher
Court of Queen's Bench, and delaying them by buy-
ing off our indispensable witness to the purchase of
the books, a compositor in Hetherington's employ, a
former apprentice of his .And here occurred two inci-
dents which may give some insight into the character
of these men, stigmatized as seditious and stirrers up
of strife, etc., as of old, it is said, were certain other
men, not altogether unlike these, in Athens and
Ephesus and elsewhere. Hetherington had determined not to pay a fine. "They might take it out
of his bones:" if not so courtly in expression, yet of
the same courage as brave Sir John Eliot's answer to
Charles I. And this martyr also had his possessions:
a shop and books, presses and other printing-

* Cleave also had been indicted, but the indictment was withdrawn on
his promise to sell no more. The others were not men to compromise.

material, besides household-stuff. Once, before all
had been swept off; he would be wiser now. Two or
three days before the trial I was with him when he
called upon the London agent of an old good friend,
Hugh Williams, a Caermarthen lawyer.* Williams
had ordered for a sufficient sum to be paid to
Hetherington, who passed the same to the hand of
one of his shopmen named Powell.† He thereupon
bought of Hetherington his whole property, brokers
being called in to value all, in order to legalize the
sale; and Hetherington, returning his friend's loan,
went penniless into Court, to meet the most that
could be inflicted. He defended himself ‡ with much
eloquence and moderation, in spite of a very bitter
and unfairly personal attack of Attorney-General
Campbell; was complimented for it by Denman, then

---

* In after days the instigator and undiscovered leader of the one
successful uprising in Britain since Cromwell,—the "Rebecca" movement in South Wales: a movement intended by him to be *educational*.
His sister, a woman of decided character and, I believe, of republican
principles, was the wife of Richard Cobden.

† THOMAS POWELL (so trusted and in that and all other respects
most worthy of trust—I need hardly say that he handed back the
property to his friend) was a Chartist like the rest of us. He too had
had his twelvemonths gaol-lesson, graduating in patriotism. Caught
for some unguarded words, which were wrested into illegal contrary
meanings, he was punished for being strong enough to hold men
back, a man more dangerous than the mere mob-inciter. After the
failure of Chartism he busied himself with organizing an emigrating
party to South America. That too, failed. He died, a few years
later, in Trinidad.

‡ The Defence he dedicated to Watson.

Chief-Justice; and sentenced to the lightest punishment upon record—imprisonment for six weeks in a debtors' prison. When he came out we were still looking for his compositor. One day walking together, Hetherington and Watson accidentally met the man; and their moral influence was sufficient to outweigh the bribe which had first tempted him. He came into Court, gave evidence, and Moxon, notwithstanding the eloquent pleading of Talfourd, was found guilty. It remained for the prosecutors to call him up for judgment, which of course was never done, personal animosity or revenge being beside the question; nor was further proceeding taken against the other indicted "blasphemers," Frazer, Richardson, and Saunders of the firm of Saunders and Ottley. We had gained enough. Prosecutions for blasphemy were stopped. I think there has since been only one, with foolish wilfulness provoked, for the sake of a spurious notoriety.

In the matter of these prosecutions, as in all other in which I had occasion to act with him, Watson's conduct commanded general respect; he knew nor undue haste nor wavering, but walked straight toward his aim as one whose will went forth to conquer; his judgment never was at fault. But for his modesty, he had all the qualities of a leader. Yet, ever unobtrusive and unassuming as he was, he led, in virtue of his quiet self-possession, his sterling good sense, his dauntless courage, and that unbounded

trust which all his associates placed in him. When
the dispute was at its highest between "physical"
and "moral," force to the needless disintegration of
the Chartist body,—when the old steadily earnest
party of Lovett and Hetherington and Watson was
outvoiced by the O'Connorites, and impulsive
Hetherington came in for his share of objurgation and
abuse, never was there an ill word or disrespectful
spoken against Watson. His calm and dignified
bearing, his justice toward all men, his well-considered
language even when most indignant, lifted him above
the reach of calumny or the intemperance of anger,
however unsparing the severity of his rebuke—never
unfairly personal—when severity became a public
duty. Strongly, sternly opposed to the empty brag-
gart speech and conduct in which our hopes of universal
suffrage were wrecked, when active patriotism
at last meaned only a mad mob howling to the praise
and glory of Feargus O'Connor and Ernest Jones
(but demagogues however well-desiring) and G. W.
M. Reynolds, the tin kettle at the mad mob's tail,—
I think there was not one of his opponents who would
have done him any harm, who did not honour
him even when most hostile. And his friends,
beyond the closer circle of his fellow-workers :—his
friends were Mazzini, and Mazzini's old comrade and
dearest of all friends, the more than noble Pole,
Stanislaus Worcell, by birth a noble, yet nobler in
exile-martyrdom; and William Bridges Adams, rail-

way engineer, a man as magnificently disinterested
as James Watson himself; and Francis Sibson,
physician, brother of the artist; and the present
Member for Newcastle on Tyne, Joseph Cowen; and
—— Surely these witnesses to character are sufficient:
else I could cite many more, dead and living, lovers
and admirers of his worth.

Some were in strong sympathy with his principles,
and so perhaps prepossessed in his favour; others,
misliking his surroundings, or without care for his
mode of action, no less esteemed the man: he had no
lack of friendship beyond the range of his political or
religious walk. Nor was he himself so narrow that
he could not work except for his special life-purpose:
not to the direct hindrance of that. Though he held
to the Charter as the one and most urgent need of
the time, and refused to accept the Reform Bill as
payment of the People's Debt, or peddle the People's
birthright for any mess of corn-law pottage, he worked
zealously for the few honest men in the Whig House
of Commons, none more actively for Duncombe and
Wakley, by the exertions of him and Moore and
of others of the same Chartist faction repeatedly returned to Parliament for the borough of Finsbury.
Mazzini's "People's International League" * had

* Formed in 1847, at the instigation and with the help of Mazzini,
in order "To enlighten the British Public as to the political condition and relations of Foreign Countries; to disseminate the principles of National Freedom and Progress; to embody and manifest
an efficient public opinion in favour of the right of every People to

his prompt adhesion, his constant attention, and his
ready subscription to the full reach of his scanty
means.   Of foreign affairs he cared to be informed ;
and the exiles, Italian, Polish, and French, found in
him an unfalteringly loyal friend.   His sympathies,
as his principles, were sure, both firmly based; and
wide. He was great-hearted, and fearless. Despising
bluster, and disliking force, if force might be
avoided,—a peaceable man, but not for peace at
whatever price,—he could not keep silence when the
men of Bradford were insurgent, but while the politic
hesitated, boldly defended their right to judge for
themselves how soon the time of patience was over
and the occasion for resistance come.   He was, as I
have already said, one of the conveners of the first
public meeting in England to congratulate the
French on their Revolution of 1848; he was on the
Committee to help the latest Polish insurrection, in
1863—4.   Latest, not last.

His own account has told us, only too briefly, of
the Fast-day in 1832: when, the country being
afflicted with cholera, an enlightened Government,
on the prescription of a certain Saint Percival, not

Self-Government and the maintenance of their own Nationality;
and to promote a good understanding between the Peoples of all
Countries."   On the list of Council stood the names of W. B. Adams,
Dr. Bowring, W. J. Fox, Goodwyn Barmby, Douglas Jerrold, T. S.
Duncombe, P. A. Taylor, P. A. Taylor junior, beside others : the
last-named, both father and son, with Moore and Watson, of the
Council also, the most active of its members.

a doctor of medicine, ordered its removal (the removal
of the cholera) by exhibition of one day's general fast
and solemn performance of prayer to Almighty God.
Performance, going through a form, says Ruskin.
Orthodox   salt-cod-and-egg-sauce   in   respectable
society—I need not pause to enumerate the necessary
accompanying wines, condiments, etc.,—seeming to
the radical and perhaps impious Association of
working-men no specific for an evil starvation-helped,
(with fifteen hundred persons in one London poor-
house—eight and ten to a bed, "from the putrid
and noxious atmosphere dying off like rotten sheep,")
these radical and so impracticable working-men refused obedience to the ministerial edict; and forbidden to work on the law-appointed holiday, nor
allowed (under old ecclesiastical law revived for the
occasion) to hold a public meeting, thought therefore
to protest in such manner as was left to them,—to
show by a quiet procession how many disapproved of
Percivalism—State-humbug, and after the walk to
provide a dinner for the poorer members of the Association. But the police obstructed and dispersed
them; and afterwards arrested the prime movers of
the procession, Watson, Lovett, and Benbow, and
had them brought to trial at the next sessions for intention to riot and breach of the peace. Of course
no one supposed it was so. The object of the prosecution was to damage the National Union through
its leaders. Twelve men, from the people, not

specially selected, are not often on the side of any tyranny in England. These, as the jury in the Calthorpe Street affair, and later in the matter of the *Poor Man's Guardian*, gave their deliberate verdict for the pubic liberties; a verdict of *Not Guilty*, after a spirited speech from each of the accused, Watson's very manly and straightforward, principally in vindication of the public right, at the same time insisting on their own peaceful conduct.

One of many witnesses voluntarily appearing to prove the peaceable, orderly behaviour of the procession was a member of the Common Council of London, Richard Taylor, a master-printer, a man of liberal views but not active in politics, highly esteemed in the city, of some note for editing Horne Tooke's *Diversions of Purley*.

On a latter occasion for protesting (in 1846, I think) another Fast-day, this time for relief of Irish famine, we had our public meeting, Watson in the chair, and from among the audience rose old Richard Taylor, to remind his friend the chairman of that former day, to congratulate him on the greater freedom we had gained, ending his unexpected speech with warm praise of him for his persistent endeavouring and for the blameless character he had maintained throughout his course.

Persistence in all that he considered right and careful avoidance of any just cause for blame were indeed characteristics of the man.

Let us look back to the prison history! In September, 1822, Watson came up to London, and spent Christmas with Carlile in jail, as foretaste of the course of instruction preparing for him in that Liberal University. Six weeks of real imprisonment before trial in the beginning of the next year, and then he remains for the full term of twelve months. Time for mature consideration out of which to shape his future life. That twelve months imprisonment was not lost upon him.

Of that year in Cold-Bath-Fields prison I have some record in his own words. He was not illtreated by his keepers; he had a room to himself; his friends were allowed to visit him at certain times; even the Governor would drop in upon him for a talk; he read much, and made notes of what he read; used his "opportunity for study and investigation; kept also some sort of diary, I fancy even more monotonous than diaries usually are. Here, however, are two entries that will interest us.

April 21, 1824—

" This day the Governor visited me. I had some of my lumber removed from the prison, as a prelude to self removal, and am not sorrowful for the circumstance. I wrote letters to friends Byerley and Driver, of Leeds, and received a letter from Mr. Carlile. The weather warm and calm."

April 22—

"This day I had all my chattels removed from the
prison, except my box. Had a long walk with Mrs.
Wright [the wife of a Leeds bookseller; in prison for
the same offence as Watson, for selling in Carlile's
shop]; drank a couple of glasses of rum-punch with
my fellow-prisoners, Mr. Humphreys and Mr. Lord
[no political sinners, one for smuggling tobacco]; the
Governor [evidently impressed in his favour] con-
gratulated me on the near termination of my imprisonment. The weather fine and warm."

Fine warm Spring weather: who does not under-
stand the freed prisoner's gladness, and the joy of
that home visit to the good, anxious mother, "to
convince her that imprisonment had not made him a
worse son." A good son surely, as sure to be a
worthy citizen! Now back to London for a liveli-
hood, in order to fulfil the duties of a citizen. But
already he is a marked man: who will employ one of
Carlile's shopmen? Let him seek work and not find,
and, wanting bread, learn the worst misery of the
proscribed! He is young. Fortunately Carlile still
needs him, will have him to conduct his business.

Perhaps his position as manager, and afterwards
his employment as compositor on the *Republican*, saved
him from another imprisonment: the governmental
raid was upon those who *sold* the publications. Then
came that kindly fever which took him to the care
of good Julian Hibbert, procuring for him his noble

friendship, finding him work until the Spring
of 1828.

He was not abandoning the cause for which he
had at first adventured. The man was unchange-
able. Though somewhile brought up under the
shadow of a shovel-hat, he had with him his mother:
a woman who would read Cobbett's "*Gridiron*" even
in a parsonage. And his first experience of punishment only set him more resolutely on the way he had
traced out for himself, for the public good. He came
to London, an unknown man, in 1822. In 1828 we
find him acting as store-keeper of the "First London
Co-operative Trading Association," in Red Lion
Square, Holborn: in the formation of which association and others similar* he had been an active helper.

In the following year he took the management of
another store, in Jerusalem Passage, Clerkenwell. In
'30 he rented a house, in Windmill Street, letting the
upper part, and retaining for his own uses only two
rooms on the ground-floor. The front room was his
shop, with a deal table for counter, on which to place
his papers and books: no trashy "light" literature

---

* The fore-runners of the more successful co-operative stores of to-day.

The first of these associations was, I believe, started at Brighton,
in 1828; and numerous others soon followed throughout the country:
the first necessary funds raised by weekly contributions of all the
members. They failed, after many trials, perhaps from many causes:
one sufficient, that there was then no legal security for such associations,—association for any purpose whatever discountenanced by the
ruling powers.

among them. The back room was his home: an old
sofa did duty for bed ; he was his own servant for all
work, preparing his own spare meals, waiting upon
himself. And here he began to print for his own
publications, when customers were not, or working
before and after the hours of business. Lowell's
words on Garrison may be applied to him :—

> " In a small chamber, friendless, and unseen,
>   Toil'd o'er his types one poor, unlearn'd young man ;
> The place was dark, unfurnitured and mean ;—
>   Yet there the freedom of a race began.

> " Help came but slowly ; surely no man yet
>   Put lever to the heavy world with less ;
> What need of help ? He knew how types were set ;
>   He had a dauntless sprit, and a press."

After a while he so far enlarged his domain as to
make room for a housekeeper, his niece, his sister's
daughter, afterwards the wife of his friend Richard
Moore.

The Fast-day prosecution was in 1832, when the
jury stood between him and a second imprisonment ;
counting preliminary six weeks in 1823 as nothing.
In '33 he was with his friend and fellow-offender
Hetherington in Clerkenwell prison : six months each
for the *Poor Man's Guardian*. This, what we call his
second prison-service, had such aggravation of punishment as is disclosed by his Petition to the " Commons ; " the deprivation of that which is most cared
for by decent men: some privacy, some mental solace
and respectable society. Subjected to the companion-

ship of the vilest and most brutal criminals, a
compelled listener to "the most horrid swearing and
the grossest licentiousness;" refused even occasional
withdrawal to the retirement of a solitary cell—[a
separate sleeping-cell, which had not been obtained
without urgent solicitation. If I mistake not, both
he and Hetherington had at the first to sleep in the
general ward]: and this suffering, this moral torture,
dread of vermin and disease superadded, was inflicted
on them illegally, under the summary jurisdiction of
police-magistrates, for selling a paper which afterwards, upon trial before a Jury, was declared to be a
publication strictly according to Law.

That six months passed ; and he was not crushed
nor converted. Only with Hibbert's legacy he began
to enlarge his publishing operations, and continued
active as ever in political and co-operative movements.

In 1834 he moved to 18, Commercial-place, City-
road—still Finsbury ; being one of the lessees and
manager of the Hall of Science, a hall near by, used
for popular meetings ; having care of that as well as
his own trade. Here, having now reached thirty-five
years of age, he on the 3rd of June brought home a
Wife, the daughter of his old (somewhile deceased)
friend Robert Byerley.

Now surely he will give up a single man's
enthusiasm, and provide first hereafter for the interests of his family and home. He is of more heroic

mould. Duty to him is (not independent of, but) higher than wife or home. And his wife is one with him : would not seduce him to play the craven. She has married him to be his helper, not his hinderer. On the 3rd of June he is married; a week later he goes with his wife to see his old bed-rid mother, eighty-two years of age, and before the end of the month is again summoned as an offender to the police-court. On the 7th of August he again enters his prison, for six months more, leaving the newly-wedded wife to manage his business during his absence. I give in her own words what here follows.

" We were married on the third of June, 1834. On the 25th he was sentenced (in his absence) for selling the *Conservative*, one of Hetherington's un-stamped papers. He left home ; stayed a week or two with Hetherington ; wrote me directions about the business, of which I then knew nothing ; and then went to Jersey, to the house of his first London friend, Thomas Hooper.*   He returned in August, and was with me for a few days. On the 7th of August two Bow-street officers arrested him : he was going along the City-road [on some election business]. They let him return a moment, to bid me farewell : and then took him to Clerkenwell Prison. I went every day but two (Sundays excepted) all the six months. It

---

* A right worthy friend ! Of whom Mrs. Watson adds, writing to me since her husband's death,—"A true, kind friend to me now ; proud of their fifty years' friendship."

was a bitter winter ; but we never met under a roof,
only in the open yard, with no seat. They let me
take him food and sheets for his loose straw bed,
which was on a shelf, in a bare stone cell ;—no fire ;—
no glass, but only bars to the windows. Some books
I took him (Lawrence's *Lectures on Physiology*, Morgan's
Philosophy of Morals,) they would not allow him to
have."

In his prison he writes to cheer the young wife :
one day, perhaps, when she can not come : a letter
that may give some glimpses of the man's nature.

"New Prison, Clerkenwell : September 12, 1834.
" My dearest Ellen ! I read and re-read your note. .
Do not suppose that my imprisonment gives me pain :
it is not that ; it is the separation from you. . . .
Never mind ! I am now recovering, and your love and
attachment will more than repay all I have endured.
I have no wish beyond that of making you happy and
endeavouring as far as possible to make the world, or
rather its inhabitants, more comfortable. I want
neither wealth nor greatness. Your confidence and
the means honestly to pay my way are the bounds of
my ambition. I care not how much I have to work,
nor for the quality or quantity of food I eat, so long
as I can keep clear of dependence upon others.
Surely we can do this. . . . .

" I am fond of home, of privacy, of books, of a
select society of friends. . . . .

" Do not let my staidness disconcert you or make

you think I am unhappy.   Remember, my dear Ellen !
what a school of adversity I have been trained in, the
obstacles I have had to encounter, the struggles I
have had to make ; to which add that my studies, by
choice—I admit, have been of a painful kind.   The
study of the cause and remedy for human woe has
engrossed all my thoughts. . . . .

"No one has stronger attachments when once
formed, . . . my Mother is to me an everlasting
affection.   She deserves it, too : yet I never could pen
those empty and heartless words that some can."

Truly a man not given to express his feelings in
many words.   A man of the puritan, or quaker stamp ;
silent and reserved save when occasion called him
out.   Then he was a ready and impressive speaker,
if not eloquent.   But if his tenderest heart-thoughts
had not words, they had the richer growth of deeds.
His loving kindnesses towards his mother and his
sister,* toward all his relations, and his wife's also,
so far as his means enabled were generously

---

* Fifteen years older than himself.   "A gentle, loving creature, very
proud of her brother ;" says the wife, writing to me lately.

By her work as a dress-maker, she helped her mother to support
him during his childhood.   She afterwards married a carpenter, on
whose earnings of fifteen shillings a week, supplemented by her own,
she had to bring up, and brought up well, a large family.   In those
expressive words of Ebenezer Elliott, a many-childed, bone-weary
woman ; a quiet quaker-like gentlewoman, as I remember her, of nice
manners, worthy of any position, of any companionship or surroundings.

manifested.—I turn back to his letters. Here is his prison life:—

"I bear my position cheerfully. See how I pass my time. I rise between eight and nine; wash and shave; breakfast, wash up my cup and saucer; walk for a time; sit down; read some instructive or amusing book; then pass a delightful hour with you; walk again; dine, and read; walk again; tea; walk a short time. Locked up in my dormitory, five feet wide by seven feet long, make my straw bed; sit down and read or write [There was no fire in his cell those winter nights.] until eleven or twelve o'clock; then think of you as I lay down for the night. Thus I pass my time. Were you with me, what would signify bolts, bars, or locks? Take care of yourself! You are to me everything."

From other letters—as manly, as affectionate, as uncomplaining, bearing witness to the bravery and gentle-heartedness of the man as well as to the worth and fortitude of the wife, I could but will not quote. So much given may be sufficient, from letters not meaned for any eyes but those of the loved and loving.

Now again be repeated those Words of a Believer: *When you see a man led to prison, or punishment, say not in your haste—This is some wicked man who has committed a crime against his fellows!*

For peradventure it is a good man——

Nay! not per adventure: through any chance or happening. This *surely is* the good man who has striven to serve his fellows, and so is punished by the oppressors.

Well, having fulfilled this third term, six months for illegal selling of the *Conservative*, he came out of prison on the twenty-first of January, 1835. Be it noted that the *Guardian*, between which and the *Conservative* there was scarcely a technical difference, had been declared a strictly legal publication in June of the preceding year. But both papers were Hetherington's, and by the aid of the technicality the authorities had their way. After this Watson was unmolested. Indeed, by Hetherington and him, and their five or six hundred assistants the Government had been defeated.

My story has been of public life and acts, with only
such glimpses of the man himself as could not but
appear in that relation. What presentment have I
given of him? Chiefly of a stern, uncompromising
antagonist, a stiffly upright stirrer of strife, hard,
obstinate, and rebellious? His enemies might have
seen him in this light: his only enemies the wrong-
doers against whom he stood. And my readers,
some perchance, may not have seen further. A plain
working-man, habited, even as he was fed and
lodged, no better than an ordinary mechanic, who
held mere finery in contempt, who would have no
luxuries of any kind, who had been ashamed of the
appearance of costliness or indulgence while men
hungered within his reach; a rigid puritan, whose
eyes were sad, whose aspect was severe, who had nor
quips nor cranks for your amusement:—Does this
describe him? His photograph without name beneath it would pass for portrait of one of Cromwell's
Ironsides. I know no modern face with more of that
seventeenth-century religiously earnest character.
But look at it again! Those sad eyes under the bent
brows are full of womanly tenderness. A smile of
kindliest benevolence, ay! and a sense of humour too,
lurks around the firm-set lips. This man, who had
not shrunk from any martyrdom,—I have seen him

fling his hat over his head and leap up as he had in
his boyhood, according to an old country superstition,
when he heard the cuckoo for the first time in Spring.
This man, the firm voice of whose severity rebuked
throned Injustice, drew the little children to his knees
by the undoubted gentleness of his inviting glance.
If he had not much fun, no word a girl should not
have heard was ever on his tongue; his manner,
though grave, was cheerful; if self-possessed and
strict, he was yet companionable; patient with
opposition; never querulous; considerate for others
in all respects; stoutly set upon his own way, but
tolerant of those who went differently; not harsh,
albeit hard against tyranny and vice. Vice of himself he knew not. If ever there was a virtuous man,
it was he. His moral conduct was irreproachable.
The white marble statue, which his life deserved,
was not more pure, more free from flaw or stain.
And let it be remarked that his youth was in the days
of George, Prince-regent, (the sty time of England)
when even the "goddess" Liberty, so lately come
from France, had something of the harlot in her
nature; when men in their extreme reaction against
repression forgot the righteousness of self-restraint,
and freedom for the sake of Order, the freedom of
the stars in their appointed courses, seemed almost
hypocrisy, or was dreaded to be a new phase of the
old Unequal Law. The wandering, the excesses,
the licentiousness of even noble men of that day

would have more excuse if their judges (of this
present generation) could realize their surroundings,
and recall the intoxication of that time of renewed
youth to Western Europe, in which the double chain
of monarchy and priestcraft was riven by France,—
though soldered since, no more to be reforged.
Days of the Saturnalia of freed slaves! The chains
now knocked off, the walk is not that of sober freemen.
To return to one for whom excuse was never needed.

Severe and self-denying as Watson was, he was
warm of heart, and generous to the full extent of his
means. Devoting all his gains to further public
services, he had little respite from his work. His
one holiday, for sake of health, was an occasional
day or, when it could be so managed, some days in
the country (for which he, born and bred there
naturally yearned), and long rambles in the fresh air
with some friend. Many an hour have we spent together
under the trees of Woodford forest, within one day's
easy reach of London; and no artist companion I
ever had more thoroughly enjoyed the scenery and
the mountain-climbs in our beautiful Lake Country
than did Watson, when, after a severe sickness, he
came to recruit with me, then living at Brantwood
(the home now of Ruskin), by Coniston-Water.
Seriously then we talked of his coming, whenever he
could withdraw from business, to live with me and
help in my republican propagandism, and the bringing out of my *English Republic*. After circumstances,

not the will of either, hindered the fulfilment of our purpose, to my loss.

I have said, the country holidays were his one enjoyment, his one recreation and rest. Not that he had not other tastes; but he spared neither time nor money for his pleasures. But after he gave up publishing he took a lodging for himself and wife in the neighbourhood of the Crystal Palace, at Norwood, so that he might daily wander among its treasures of art and manufacture, and hear the music. I go back to earlier times.

Three years, including the prison time, he rented the house in Commercial-place; then for a year he found it more convenient to occupy the lower rooms of the Hall of Science. From there he removed across the street to 15, City-road. In 1843 he had a shop at 5, Paul's Alley, and afterwards at 3, Queen's Head Passage, Paternoster Row, where I find him some eleven years later, the date of the testimonial. The upper part of the house in the Passage he had, however, let, retaining only the shop for his own use; and had for some two or three years been living, in easier circumstances but simply as of old, at 17, Thornhill Terrace (127 Hemingford-road), Islington. Here he continued to reside until, I think, 1865 or '66, when he went to Norwood, to be within walking reach of the Crystal Palace. Though out of business he still retained his interest in the old questions of freedom of opinion; and if as years passed by they

found him less active than heretofore, the cause lay
in the years themselves,—the stagnant years that
succeeded a period of so great excitement. There
was no let or deadening of his patriotic and philanthropic zeal; the man was yet ready if opportunity
had invited or occasion called him forth. He aided
his friend Moore, throughout the prolonged struggle,
for an absolutely untaxed Press; * and was, as said
before, one of the Committee of sympathizers with
unhappy Poland in 1864. His devoted love of
Liberty, the Liberty which is the right of growth,
knew no abatement; and the old man, nearing the
term of three-score and ten years, was young at heart.

The evening of his life was worthy of the morning.
Happy in his home with a wife who loved and
honoured him; loved and honoured too by many
friends; in fair health (though tried in earlier years);
with an income (not greater indeed than a day-
labourer's) sufficient for his simple needs and all his
own earning, his books and leisure, and outside
opportunities of enjoyment: he had the well-deserved
reward of all his conscientious work, his self-denial
and devotedness for the good of others. Day by day

---

* Some idea may be had of the labour here involved when I state,
on Collet's authority, that the Committee of which Moore was
chairman [appointed by the People's Charter Union as the
"Newspaper (*penny*) Stamp Abolition Committee," afterwards
Committee of the Association for repeal of all the taxes on
knowledge,] from its formation, in 1849, to the abolition of the
duty on paper, in 1861, had to meet 473 times.

there was his walk to the Palace, and hours of quiet pleasure, viewing and examining the marvels of art and science here stored.   More than all, there was a never-failing delight in the frequent concerts. Knowing not a note of music, he yet had a liking for the best.   He would come home and say—"I am late, but we had a selection from Handel (or from Mozart or Beethoven) on the Grand Organ, and I could not but stay to hear it."   Sometimes the wife accompanied him.   Often too he would meet old friends,—it might be by accident, it might be they had come with purpose to see and spend some hours with him.   But he was no less happy alone.   So passed the next five or six years.

A severe sickness of his wife, in 1872, first broke him down.   Fear for her, anxiety and exertion, over-taxed his strength.   When, returning from America, I last saw him, in 1872-3, he was suffering from in-tensest melancholy without apparent cause, and fail-ing fast.   Winter of 1873-4 he stayed at Blaydon-on-Tyne, at the house of Joseph Cowen, who, and his wife also, esteemed and loved him ; and their careful kindness seemed to revive him.   Helped further by a journey into Wales with his old friend Hooper, he rallied for a while.   It was only for a while.   The sadness returned.   Still he would go to the Palace : the music cheered him.   But the fire of life was flickering out.   Some days of wavering memory, one week in bed,—and the weary had found his rest :

passing away in his sleep, without a struggle, without a sigh. He died on the twenty-ninth of November, 1874, at Burns Cottage, Hamilton-road, Lower Norwood; and was buried in Norwood Cemetery.——A plain granite obelisk erected over the grave, through the ready action of an old Chartist comrade, Joseph W. Corfield, marks the spot where sleeps that " noblest work of God "—

AN HONEST MAN.

On the grey granite obelisk is the following inscription:

JAMES WATSON

1874

ERECTED BY A FEW FRIENDS AS A TOKEN OF REGARD

FOR HIS INTEGRITY OF CHARACTER

AND HIS BRAVE EFFORTS TO SECURE

THE RIGHT OF FREE SPEECH

AND

A FREE AND UNSTAMPED PRESS

And on a square block of polished red granite beneath:

IN MEMORY OF

JAMES WATSON

PUBLISHER

Born Sept. 21, 1799—Died Nov. 29, 1874.

Gentle as brave he shunn'd no duteous strife
To help his fellow men opposing wrong.
Scorning reward, he freely spent his life ;
And made of all his days a patriot song.

In personal appearance Watson was not remarkable: he would not have been spoken of as handsome, though he was well-made and well-featured, and of goodly stature,—his passport says—" height 5 feet, 8 inches" (I would have said taller), and "light complexion, blue eyes and brown hair;" square-shouldered, and firmly but sparely made, certainly no tendency to corpulence. His head square and well set; his features regular; till late in life close-shaven. In the latter years he let his beard grow. In ordinary talk his manner was generally serious, earnest always, his matter weighty and sincere; the tone of his voice was pleasant, his words were correct and well-spoken: sometimes with those nearest to him, or when moved, recurring to the Yorkshire old country form, yet used, the quaker *thou* and *thee*, instead of *you*. On the platform his bearing was simple, dignified, earnest, and impressive, and without gestures; his speech unhesitating but deliberate, well chosen-words clearly enunciated, and sound argument. No oratorical display, but straight-hitting strong good sense delivered direct from the heart. He seemed always, and in private as well as public, to have before him the ideal of what an English workman ought to be [I think of him always as a workman, because, though he had a shop, he was in no sense a tradesman—a buyer and seller for gain], not through any priggish assump-

tion born of introspective formality. Too healthy a
man to require continual self-probing, he grew as a
tree, in worthiness, though using his human reason
in training and pruning for more certain growth.

Of his political opinions there is little need to
speak, after all already told. They may be summed
up as of the school of Paine, those writings have been,
and still are, the political Gospel of our English
working classes. The more philosophical views of
the French revolutionists, whatever additional
impulse they have given, were never so well digested
by the masses as the plainer common sense of their
own countryman. French teachings rather had issue
in the thoughts of the more scholarly of English politicians, an indirect rather than a direct influence
upon English action.

On his religious meditations I do not care to
intrude. Such speculations, so far as they concern
only the man himself, it seems to me are no concern
of any one else. Had he been questioned, I think he
might have replied in the words of Paine—*To do good
is my religion;* and have found sufficient ground for
action in these of good old John Woolman—*Whoever
rightly advocates the good of some thereby promotes the good
of the whole.* I would imgaine (I do not recollect to
have heard him say) that his faith was much the same
as Paine's : a simple belief in some over-ruling Power
which leads the harmony of the Universe,—whence
he deducted his maxim of duty, toward which he

could not but square his life, uncaring for any bribe of "heaven," nor needing to be driven by dread of "hell." I do not know that he troubled himself about particular providences, or essayed to fathom the Infinite, in order to justify the ways of God; but I do know that he had a clear perception of righteousness and the Higher Law, to which he reverently bowed his life in daily and hourly worship. Of course I am aware that "only this" takes him from the pale of Christianity and relegates him to the glorious company of "Infidels." Which may not matter much. As he cared not to talk of what thoughtful speculations stirred his soul, I shall not pretend to speak concerning them, but rather leave his religion with this report, indefinite or precise according to the reader's judgment. For myself, I learned his faith snfficiently from his work.

His favourite poem was Bryant's *Thanatopsis*: it may he because expressing his own as calm contemplation of death as rest after a well spent life. To look for glory or reward was not a necessity for one whose work was reward enough. The last books he read were Forster's Lives of *Sir John Eliot* and *Goldsmith* (Goldsmith but a few days before the end): characteristic of himself,—brave and conscientious as the first, and gentle-hearted as the other.

He was not a man of genius; he did not care to make a name; he had "no ambition for authorship." Yet he deserved the oaken crown. I never before considered whether he had or had not genius.   In the presence of his integrity of life it seems a question altogether unrequired.   God forbid that I should de-preciate genius !   Assuredly do I recognise in the flashes of a Byron or a Burns the wondrous lightnings of the Eternal.   But in the steady life-splendour of one who never faltered, who never swerved from right, whose careful thought was always obeyed by corres-ponding deeds, whose word was his bond, whose record is without stain—I perceive—if not the excep-tional fire of heaven—the clear common daylight, in which the Highest is revealed to us, as by the pillar of flame, to guide or cheer us on our way.

It has been my rare fortune to have as friends and to be intimate with many noble men : the greatest of this age—of the ages, Joseph Mazzini,—the Polish martyr, Worcell,—the Russian patriot, Herzen,—the venerable Lamennais,—William Bridges Adams,—Leigh Hunt, beside artist comrades close and dear, Thomas Sibson, Edward Wehnert, Alfred Stephens, and some yet living :—but of no man's friendship am I more proud than of the forty years friendship of JAMES WATSON.

With what more words shall I conclude ?   I can find none fitter to my own feelings than those I wrote on first hearing of his death: printed in the New York *Evening Post*, afterwards in England, in the *Newcastle Chronicle*.

ONCE more the Powers have taken hence
  Their own.   Why fall our tears?
Who gave resume!   O vain defence
  Of slowly fading years!

How many noble Englishmen,
  Death! hast thou in thy fold:
Their legends writ with firmest pen
  On History's tombs of gold?

Yet he, whom thou hast gather'd now,
  May rank among thy best,
Though passing with unlaurell'd brow
  Unnoticed to his rest.

To-day is come and will depart,—
  To-morrow none will say—
From English life our truest heart
  So lately passed away.

Only an obscure workman he,
  Poor without place of birth:
Yet born to make his country free
  By energy of worth.

O peerless Milton! flawless Vane!
  We miss you doubly now,—
Your thought in him lived once again
  The same undaunted brow

Was his before the front of Power,
　　The same unprison'd soul,
The same clear sight beyond the hour
　　To see the further goal.

The same integrity of life:
　　He gave it without stint;
And loving peace, yet sought the strife
　　At Duty's lightest hint.

A man who knew not how to lie—
　　He knew not how to fear:
Upright in his firm honesty,
　　And loving as sincere.

A patriot, strict to private due;
　　Severe, and yet so sweet;
So glad a nature, his smile drew
　　The children round his feet.

O poorly rear'd, as lowly born!
　　When thy sad eyes are dim
Before the uplifted hand of Scorn,
　　Point thou beyond to him.

O Labour's bondslaves, who would claim
　　The freeman's fitter place!
Write in your hearts this labourer's name
　　Whose life brought labour grace;

Who made his work a poem grand,
  No poet's words more high ;
Who dared and suffered to withstand
  Thy spoilers, Industry !

Not asking for himself reward
  Of praise or worldly part ;
Still giving, from the exhaustless hoard
  Of his most royal heart.

Brave as the bravest Ironside,
  Yet gentlest of the brave——
O Friend ! like thee to have lived and died
  Were worth a noteless grave.

Knowing the world's forgetfulness of those who have passed out of sight, I did not when writing those lines expect a monument to be raised to him ; nor think until asked by Mrs. Watson of writing this Memoir. Would that it more fully represented my love for him ; would that it were worthier of the man !

THE END.

IN THE PRESS.

THE LIFE AND WORKS

of the late

JOHN CRITCHLEY PRINCE,

IN THREE VOLUMES, FIFTEEN SHILLINGS.

MANCHESTER :

Abel Heywood and Son, Oldham Street.

POEMS OF THE LATE CHARLES SWAIN.

THE MIND AND OTHER POEMS,

Cloth, 2/-.

DRYBURGH ABBEY AND OTHER POEMS,

Limp Cloth, 1/-.

SONGS AND BALLADS,

Limp Cloth, 1/-.

MANCHESTER:

Abel Heywood and Son, Oldham Street.

LANCASHIRE WORTHIES,

BY

FRANCIS ESPINASSE,

With a Portrait of Humphrey Chetham, being memoirs of distinguished men of the county, from the age of Richard III. to that of George III.

Price, Cloth, 3/6.

MANCHESTER :
Abel Heywood and Son, Oldham Street.

APPENDIX

This four page catalogue was issued by Watson somewhere around 1840. Its contents indicate the range of titles that he published or sold in the decade or so after his entry into printing and publishing in 1831. Both Thomas Paine and Robert Owen are, as one might expect, well represented. Prices vary considerably, and the value of the catalogue lies in the fact that it shows exactly what the leading radical publisher and bookseller at this period offered his customers.

In general, the catalogue and advertisements of radical, Chartist, freethinking publishers and booksellers have not yet been the subject of serious inquiry. A brief examination of a number of these lists made over a period of years by the present writer reveals the existence at one time of a vast sub-literature, some of which may indeed not have survived; but if the quality and extent of nineteenth century political and freethinking activity at grass roots level are to be assessed, it must be taken into account.

It is not difficult to imagine the prejudice against "progressive" publications which existed in the last century. How then did working men buy the magazines, books and pamphlets which they wanted? There were booksellers like William Goddard of John Street, Fitzroy Square, who specialised in such sales during the eighteen fifties; and a book canvasser, Joseph Bowker travelled a circuit twenty miles round Huddersfield and advertised in 1854 that he was prepared to take orders for publications by "authors on the side of Religious Progress".

If the study of literacy in nineteenth century society is to be made something more than merely a rising graph upon a statistical table—if we are to discover what the working classes read, and how they obtained what they wanted—then it becomes necessary to look closely at the book trade. More specifically, it is vital to examine those areas of it which were not dominated by John Murray, Richard Bentley, the Tinsley Brothers, nor by remaindersmen like Thomas Tegg, but rather, for example, by Richard Carlisle, Abel Heywood, G. T. Holyoake and of course, James Watson.

LIST OF BOOKS,

SOLD WHOLESALE AND RETAIL BY

J. WATSON, 5, PAUL'S ALLEY,

Opposite the Chapter Coffee House, one door from Paternoster Row.

———————

J. W. announces to his friends and the public that he has taken a shop in the above central situation, where all works of a liberal character, either on politics or theology, are kept constantly on sale. Wholesale and retail Orders punctually attended to either in town or country.—*Terms, Cash only.*

———————

Just published, Vol. 1, price Three Shillings, cloth boards, and lettered,
ENQUIRY CONCERNING POLITICAL JUSTICE
And its Influence on Morals and Happiness. By William Godwin. To be had also in Five Parts at Sixpence each, or in Fifteen Numbers at Twopence each.

N.B. The Second Volume is in course of publication, in Parts and numbers.

	s.	d.
Poems by Robert Nicoll, with an interesting Sketch of his Life, 1 vol.	5	0
Mirabaud's System of Nature, 2 vols. cloth bds. and lettered	7	6
To be had in Parts at Sixpence and in Numbers at Twopence.		
Discussion on the Existence of God and the Authenticity of the Bible, between Origen Bacheler and Robert Dale Owen, 1 vol. cloth boards and lettered	4	6
Discussion on the Authenticity of the Bible, between O. Bacheler and R. D. Owen, 1 vol. cloth boards, lettered ...	3	2
Ditto, in a wrapper	2	8
Discussion on the Existence of God, between O. Bacheler and R. D. Owen, 1 vol. cloth boards and lettered	1	10
Ditto, in a wrapper	1	4
To be had also in Eight Parts, at Sixpence each, or in Twenty-four Numbers, at Twopence each.		
Volney's Ruins of Empires and Law of Nature; 1 vol. cloth boards and lettered, with Three Engravings	3	0
To be had in Parts at Sixpence, and in Numbers at Twopence each.		
Volney's Lectures on History, cloth boards	1	6
Ditto, in a wrapper	1	0
Volney's Law of Nature	0	4
Sketch of the Life of Volney	0	2
Miss Wright's Popular Lectures, 1 vol. cloth boards and lettered	3	0
To be had in Parts at Sixpence each, or in Numbers at Twopence each.		
Miss Wright's Few Days in Athens, cloth boards and lettered	1	6
Ditto, in a wrapper	1	0
Miss Wright's Fables	0	3

PAINE'S WORKS.

Paine's Theological Works, 1 vol. cloth boards and lettered.	3	0
To be had in Numbers at Twopence each, and in Parts at Sixpence each.		
Paine's Political Works, vol. 1, cloth boards and lettered ...	3	0
Ditto, vol. 2	3	0

To be had in separate pamphlets, as follows—

Paine's American Crisis, in a wrapper	1	6
—— Rights of Man, ditto	1	3
—— Common Sense, ditto	0	6
—— Letter to the Abbé Raynal, ditto	0	6
—— Letters to the Citizens of the United States of America, ditto	0	4
—— Public Good, ditto	0	4
—— Decline and Fall of the English System of Finance ...	0	3
—— Agrarian Justice, ditto	0	2
—— Dissertation on First Principles of Government, ditto	0	2
—— Reply to the Bishop of Llandaff, ditto	0	2
—— Letter to Camille Jordan, on Priests, Bells, and Public Worship	0	1
—— Discourse to the Society of Theophilanthropists at Paris	0	1
—— Life, by the Editor of the National	0	6
—— Portrait, engraved on Steel, Proofs	1	0
Ditto, Plain	0	6

P. B. Shelley's Queen Mab; a philisophical poem, complete, with all the Notes, 1 vol. cloth boards	1	6
Ditto, in a wrapper	1	0
—————— Masque of Anarchy, &c. &c. with a Preface by Leigh Hunt	0	3
Sketch of the Life of P. B. Shelley	0	2

TRACTS BY ROBERT DALE OWEN—

Influence of the Clerical Profession	0	3
Republican Government and National Education	0	3
Sermons on Loyalty, Free Inquiry, &c.	0	3
Hopes and Destinies of the Human Species	0	2
Address on Free Inquiry	0	2
Darby and Susan: a tale of Old England	0	2
Wealth and Misery	0	2
Situations: Lawyers, Clergy, Physicians, Men, and Women.	0	2
Galileo and the Inquisition	0	2
Lecture on Consistency	0	2
Prossimo's Experience, &c. &c.	0	2
The above Tracts can be had in 1 vol. neat cloth boards ...	2	6
R. D. Owen's Moral Physiology; a brief and plain treatise on the Population Question	0	6

The National; a useful collection of original and selected matter in favour of Liberty and Free Inquiry; illustrated by 27 Wood Engravings, 1 vol. 8vo., cloth boards and lettered	5	0
To be had also in Parts, and in Numbers.		
Essays on the Formation and Publication of Opinions, 1 vol. cloth boards and lettered	3	0

Palmer's Principles of Nature, cloth boards, lettered	2	0
Ditto ditto, in a wrapper	1	6
To be had in Nine Numbers, at Twopence each.		
Bailey's Monthly Messenger; a repository of information, 1 vol. cloth boards	3	0
To be had in Ten Numbers, at Threepence each.		
Carpenter's Political Text Book, 1 vol. cloth boards	2	6
Clark's Letters to Dr. Adam Clarke, on the Life, Miracles, &c. of Jesus Christ, 1 vol. cloth boards	5	0
Bible of Reason, 1 vol. cloth boards and lettered	7	0
Buonarotti's History of Babeuf's Conspiracy for Equality, 1 vol. cloth boards	4	0
To be had in Twenty Numbers at Twopence each.		
Bronterre's Life of Robespierre, vol. 1, cloth boards	6	0
To be had in Parts at One Shilling, or in Numbers at Three-pence each.		
The New Ecce Homo, 1 vol. cloth boards	3	0
Rev. R. Taylor's Diegesis, 1 vol. cloth boards	10	0
Lawrence's Lectures on Physiology, Zoology, and the Natural History of Man, 12 plates, 1 vol. boards	4	6
Mackintosh's Electrical Theory of the Universe, 1 vol. cloth boards	6	0
To be had in Numbers at Threepence each.		
Mackintosh on the Being and Attributes of God	0	8
Mackintosh on Responsibility	1	4
To be had in Numbers at Threepence each.		
Life and Beauties of Pemberton	0	3
Strauss' Life of Jesus, 1 vol.	3	9
To be had in Numbers at Three halfpence.		
Owen's Six Lectures on the Evils of the existing State of Society, cloth boards	1	6
Ditto, in a wrapper	1	0
Carpenter's Life of Milton, 1 vol. cloth boards	3	6
Howitt's Popular History of Priestcraft, abridged, 1 vol. bds.	1	6
Owen and Roebuck's Discussion, 1 vol. cloth boards	2	0
The Rational School Grammar. By W. Hill	1	0
Progressive Exercises. By W. Hill	1	0
The Grammatical Text Book. By W. Hill	0	6
Fifteen Lessons on the Analogy and Syntax of the English Language	2	0

Dr. Smyles' Letter to Mr. Pitkethly, on the subject of Emi-gration to the United States, with the writer's Observa-tions on the Government, &c. &c. Also, on the fitness of Wisconsin as a Residence for English Emigrants	0	1
The Protestant's Progress, from Church-of-Englandism to Infidelity; or reasons for declining to attend Public Wor-ship, in a Letter to a Priest of the Church of England. With additional Notes and Illustrations. By Rees Grif-fith, esq.	1	0
The Doubts of Infidels	0	3
An Essay on the Functions of the Brain	0	2
Ædipus Judaicus of Sir W. Drummond, Preface to	0	1
Diderot's Thoughts on Religion	0	1
Socialism Made Easy. By C. Southwell	0	2

Books published at 5, Paul's Alley, Paternoster Row.

The People Armed against Priestcraft	0	8
Hume's Essay on Miracles	0	3
Right of Free Discussion. By Thomas Cooper, M.D.	0	3
Important Examination of the Holy Scriptures. By M. de Voltaire	0	6
Sketch of the Life of Voltaire	0	2
Sketch of the Life of the Baron D'Holbach	0	2
On Removing Hirelings from the Church, by John Milton	0	6
On the Liberty of the Press, by ditto	0	6
Death-Bed Repentance. By Cooper	0	2
Chartism. By Lovett and Collins	1	0
Modern Slavery. By the Abbe de la Mennais	0	4
The Rotten House of Commons	0	3
Speech of Robert Emmett	0	1
Vision of Judgment. By Lord Byron	0	3
Ditto. By R. Southey	0	2
Wat Tyler. By ditto	0	2
Life of Robert Emmett	1	0
Poor Man's Book of the Church	0	6
Notes on the Population Question. By Anti-Marcus	0	6
Fruits of Philosophy. By C. Knowlton, M.D.	0	6
Portrait of Mary Wolstonecraft Godwin	0	3
———— William Godwin	0	3

Economy of Human Life, cloth bds.	0	6
Bloomfield's Poems	0	3
Catechism of the Corn Laws	0	1
Sir James Mackintosh's Vindiciæ Gallicæ, being a Defence of the French Revolution of 1789, 1 vol. cloth boards	1	4
The Constitution of Society as Designed by God; one large volume, bds. published at 15s.	5	0
Shelley's Revolt of Islam, 1 vol. bds.	2	0
Voltaire's Philosophical Dictionary, 6 vols. bds.	25	0
The Law of Reason, 1 vol. half bound	3	0
The Life of Henry Hunt, Esq. 2 vols. cloth lettered	4	0
Laborde's History of Spain, 5 vols	6	0
Sir C. T. Morgan's Philosophy of Life	3	0
Mary Wolstonecraft on the French Revolution	3	6
F. Hill, on National Education, 2 vols.	3	6
Mirabaud's Letters De Cachett, 2 vols.	3	0
Paley's Natural Theology Illustrated. By Lord Brougham, 1 vol.	3	0
Byron's Don Juan, 1 vol.	2	0
Burke's Reflections on the French Revolution, 1 vol.	1	
The Pocket Lacon, 1 vol.	2	0
Sterne's Works, 1 large vol. cloth lettered	7	6
Essays on Miscellaneous Subjects. By J. N. Bailey, 1 vol.	2	3
The Social Hymn Book	1	6
Sir R. Phillips on the Proximate Causes of Phenomena, 1 vol.	5	0
The Social System. By John Gray, 1 vol.	3	6
H. B. Fearon, on Materialism, Religious Festivals, and Sabbaths, 1 vol.	2	6
The Cottage Gardener. By T. Poynter	0	8
Frances Wright's Travels in America	3	6